Hammered

Young people and alcohol

By Fast Forward Positive Lifestyles

Russell House Publishing

First published in 2005 by:
Russell House Publishing Ltd.
4 St. George's House
Uplyme Road
Lyme Regis
Dorset DT7 3LS
Tel: 01297-443948
Fax: 01297-442722
e-mail: help@russellhouse.co.uk
www.russellhouse.co.uk

British Library Cataloguing-in-publication Data:
A catalogue record for this book is available from the British Library.

ISBN: 1-903855-51-9

Design and layout by Jeremy Spencer. Insert designed by Keith Clark.

Printed by Cromwell Press, Trowbridge.

About Russell House Publishing

RHP is a group of social work, probation, education and youth and community work practitioners and academics working in collaboration with a professional publishing team. Our aim is to work closely with the field to produce innovative and valuable materials to help managers, trainers, practitioners and students. We are keen to receive feedback on publications and new ideas for future projects. For details of our other publications please visit our website or ask us for a catalogue. Contact details are on this page.

Contents

Introduction

Alcohol is a widely available, socially acceptable, legal drug. Whether we consume it ourselves or not, we cannot ignore the central place it occupies in many societies and the significant role it plays in global economic activity.

Its use brings with it a wide range of consequences, not the least of which are the detrimental effects that excessive use can have on physical and mental health. Alcohol consumption also has strong links with exclusion from school, unsafe sexual health practices, mental health problems, anti-social behaviour and crime, ranging from driving while intoxicated to child abuse and murder.

Alcohol and young people

In many countries of the world there are significant legal restrictions on the sale of alcohol to children and young people. In theory this should mean that children and young people should not experience the impact of alcohol until they reach adulthood. However, this is often not the case. Children and teenagers consume alcohol for many different reasons, sometimes with, but more often without adult permission. In addition the drinking habits of others can have significant impact on their lives, such as parents or carers who become abusive through drink.

Alcohol education

Alcohol can have the most damaging and far-reaching consequences for children and young people and alcohol education has an important role in addressing the impact of its use.

Accordingly, those of us who have extended contact with young people through our paid or voluntary work with them can have an important role to play in putting the facts in front of them. Some may be lucky enough to work in partnership with specialists from either health or community safety agencies, but *Hammered* aims to help you in the frequent circumstances when such help is not available.

This teaching pack tackles a wide range of alcohol related topics. It contains factual information we should all know, but sometimes overlook, and suggests techniques of passing this knowledge on to the young people we work with in an informative, and often, fun way. *Hammered* is designed to support you as a practitioner to feel confident in delivering alcohol education with young people aged 10 to 25. It will help you engage with them at their level and deal appropriately with the issues relevant to them. It offers help with breaking the ice, passing on information, challenging attitudes and developing problem solving skills.

Who is Hammered for?

Hammered has been designed to be of value to a whole range of workers and volunteers with diverse backgrounds and varying levels of experience who are working with young people today. It does not claim to be completely comprehensive nor trail blazingly innovative, however, it will provide the basics of alcohol information and give practical help with informal education to help you get started in the often confusing field of health education.

Hammered will be of use to:
- Workers who are new to youth work.
- Those who feel they need more alcohol knowledge.
- Those who want a confidence boost to deliver health education to young people.

This manual usefully pulls together examples of good practice in a way that will save busy workers time, help you reflect on your own practice and encourage you to build your own resources. It contains many tried and tested games and exercises some of which the more experienced practitioner will recognise. All in all, it is a manual to dip in and out of. Use what is relevant to you.

What? Nothing new here then?

Some readers of this manual will recognise materials that Fast Forward originally published in an earlier manual called *Skoosh*. We were delighted at the encouraging feedback and positive sales which that manual generated, however ongoing conversations with practitioners in this field over the last five years have shown that this work has moved on:
- Many workers and organisations have asked for assistance in developing and running mixed gender alcohol education programmes.
- Both central and local government are promoting initiatives which tackle alcohol misuse.
- Police forces and the media are expressing concern about the increasing numbers of underage drinkers.

We felt the time was right to publish an up-to-date manual to meet the needs of today's worker delivering alcohol education to young people.

So what is in this manual?

Hammered is a comprehensive resource designed to help you feel confident, in working with 'your' young people around the issues of alcohol. It contains:
- Enough **factual alcohol information** to enable the practitioner to run a comprehensive education programme including statistical information on alcohol's impact on health and crime.
- **Techniques and materials** that will support you in passing on that information to young people. Extensive examples of practical groupwork exercises – and numerous photocopiable resources, including two fun quizzes – will help you address issues such as gender, drinking patterns, role models, cultural differences, and the law. Intensely practical, all the material has been tried and tested in various formal and informal settings with male, female and mixed gender groups.
- **Guidance** in devising your programme to de-mystify and build confidence by assisting those who are new to planning and delivering health education work.
- **Helpful resources** contact details for further information and advice on alcohol issues, dependency or ethnic minority groups.
- Tucked inside the back cover of the manual is a copy of Fast Forward's **Hammered** leaflet. An alcohol education resource produced by young people, for young people, telling 'a tale of drink, sex and violence'. It is in cartoon form, drawn by Keith Clark, and doubles as a two-sided poster with *Alcohol Affects Everybody* on the back. It can be used as a straight forward information resource or as a tool in your education programme. Further copies are available from Fast Forward.

Hammered
Young people and alcohol

We hope that workers with all levels of experience and expertise will find something here to expand their work with young people. Alcohol is a powerful substance whose dangers can all too easily be overlooked because it is legal, so widely available and so commonly used. For those of us who have contact with sometimes impressionable and vulnerable young people, the provision of quality health education is a vital and important role. *Hammered* can be used to support you in this role, as a complete training manual, or as a 'dip-in' resource.

Although the focus of this publication is predominantly on work with young people, Fast Forward recognises the importance of alcohol education with all age ranges and many of the activities provided can be adapted and used to address alcohol issues with adult groups.

Fast Forward has been working in the field of substance education since 1987 and are committed to gathering and disseminating good practice. If you would like to talk about your work, comment on the manual or would like more structured and longer-term consultation we can be contacted at:

Fast Forward Positive Lifestyles Ltd.
4 Bernard Street
Edinburgh
EH6 6PP
Tel: 0131 554 4300
admin@fastforward.org.uk

Section 1

Alcohol information

This section is designed to provide enough information for you to run a well informed alcohol education programme and although brief, it is comprehensive. However, there is no shortage of other resources and reference materials that can add to your knowledge and some suggested sources can be found at the end of the chapter.

What is alcohol?

Alcohol is a word that describes a whole group of chemicals rather than just a single substance. The one that we drink and call 'alcohol' is actually ethyl alcohol.

It is produced, along with carbon dioxide, when yeast ferments sugars. A whole range of natural sugar sources can be fermented to produce the wide variety of alcoholic drinks that we humans consume now. Different parts of the world produce different alcoholic drinks depending upon the type of sugar sources available locally. Grain for beer and whisky grow better in Northern Europe while grapes for wine and brandy fare better in the warmer climes around the Mediterranean. Other raw materials that are fermented in various parts of the world include potatoes for vodka, apples for cider and sugar cane for rum.

Alcohol is a *depressant* drug. In physiological terms, it slows down both the heart and respiratory rate. It also has a huge effect on brain function. Loss of inhibitions and feelings of elation come from the initial effects of alcohol on the part of the brain that controls behaviour. This is why alcohol is often wrongly believed to be a stimulant.

When under the influence we often behave outrageously or take things further than we would normally. Alcohol suppresses our natural caution, fear and restraint.

The body

There are several factors that influence how alcohol will affect a person. These include age, gender, physical condition, amount of food eaten and the effect of other drugs or medicines taken.

Alcohol is poisonous to the human tissues. To counter this, the body produces at least nine different forms of an enzyme known as alcohol dehydrogenase (ADH) which metabolises the alcohol and allows it to be safely processed and excreted by the body. The ADH enzymes begin converting the alcohol into other substances in the stomach; however the bulk of the breakdown takes place in the liver. Less than ten per cent of alcohol is dealt with by the kidneys, lungs and via sweat.

A healthy liver can process about one unit (see below) of alcohol per hour, so if you have two pints of average strength beer (i.e. four units) at lunchtime and went back to the pub three hours later, there would still be alcohol left in your blood. Whatever alcohol you drink at your second sitting will be added to what is still left in your system. You would not have been sober since before your lunchtime drinks.

Some people believe that drinking black coffee or having a cold shower will sober them up. This is not true, only time and your liver function will sober you up.

Alcohol causes dehydration. Recognising alcohol as a toxin, your body will remove water from your cells to help flush it from your body. The more you drink the more water is needed to help flush it out. Hangovers are a result of too much water being removed from the body because you have drunk excessively, not by mixing drinks. Drinking water during and after drinking helps prevent the excessive dehydration of your cells and consequently hangover symptoms. But the best way to avoid a hangover is to drink less alcohol or abstain completely. Some drinks, for example, the darker ones such as red wine, sherry, port, beer etc. will give you a worse one. This is because they have a higher content of congeners. These are the additives which give colour and taste to alcohol.

The body starts to absorb alcohol within five to ten minutes by absorbing it into the bloodstream through the wall of the small intestine. How much alcohol you have in your blood will depend on what you are drinking and how quickly you drink it. The amount of food in your stomach will also influence how quickly the alcohol gets into your body. Consuming a glass of wine with a meal will take more time to get into your blood stream and consequently produce effects, than a neat whisky on an empty stomach. The process of absorption is however speeded up by fizzy mixers and by the bubbles in sparkling wines.

With continued excessive use the body will develop a tolerance to alcohol and become reliant on it in order to function with a degree of normality. To get that drunken feeling more and more alcohol will have to be consumed to achieve the same effect. Not drinking at all at this stage, may trigger withdrawal symptoms such as shaking, sweating and not being able to think clearly.

Alcohol has a lot of calories for very little nutritional effect, so a heavy drinker may be overweight and suffer from malnutrition. The alcohol will provide lots of calories but no essential vitamins and minerals. Alcohol can in fact stop the absorption of essential vitamins and minerals if it is consumed in excess.

Alcohol dependence

If you are 'alcohol dependent' you have a strong desire for alcohol and have difficulty in controlling your drinking. In addition, your body is so used to lots of alcohol that you start to develop withdrawal symptoms 3-8 hours after your last drink, as the effect of the alcohol wears off. 'Withdrawal' symptoms include: feeling sick, trembling, sweating, craving for alcohol, and feeling unwell. You need to keep drinking to prevent these symptoms which makes giving it up difficult.

The severity of dependence can vary. It can develop gradually and become more severe. You may be developing alcohol dependence if you:
- Need a drink every day.
- Drink alone often.
- Need a drink to stop trembling (the shakes).
- Drink early, or first thing in the morning (to avoid withdrawal symptoms).
- Often have a strong desire to drink alcohol.
- Spend a lot of your time in activities where alcohol is available and you drink, such as socialising in the pub or social club.
- Neglect other interests or pleasures because of alcohol drinking.

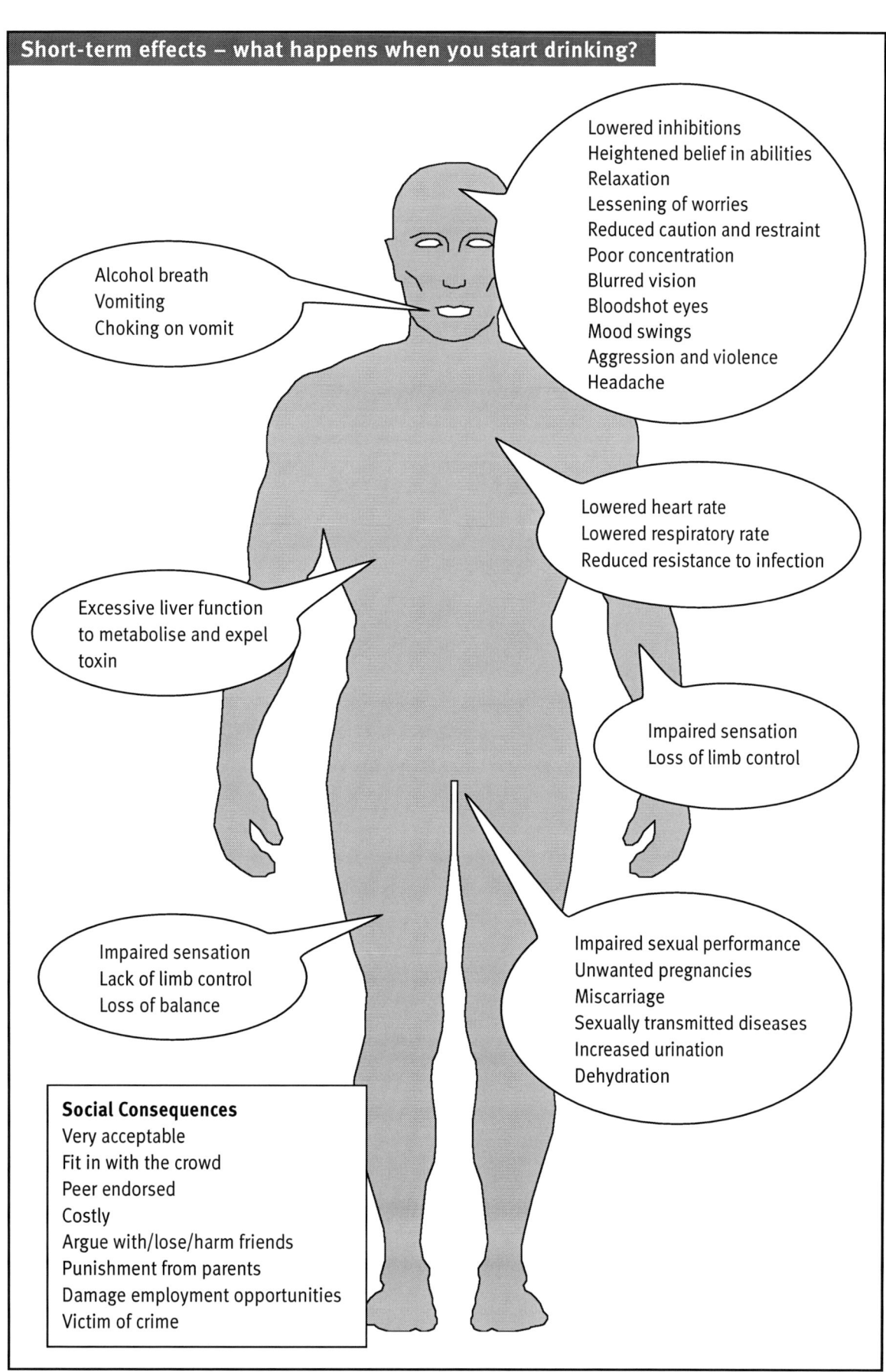

Alcohol breath
Vomiting
Choking on vomit

Lowered inhibitions
Heightened belief in abilities
Relaxation
Lessening of worries
Reduced caution and restraint
Poor concentration
Blurred vision
Bloodshot eyes
Mood swings
Aggression and violence
Headache

Lowered heart rate
Lowered respiratory rate
Reduced resistance to infection

Excessive liver function
to metabolise and expel
toxin

Impaired sensation
Loss of limb control

Impaired sensation
Lack of limb control
Loss of balance

Impaired sexual performance
Unwanted pregnancies
Miscarriage
Sexually transmitted diseases
Increased urination
Dehydration

Social Consequences
Very acceptable
Fit in with the crowd
Peer endorsed
Costly
Argue with/lose/harm friends
Punishment from parents
Damage employment opportunities
Victim of crime

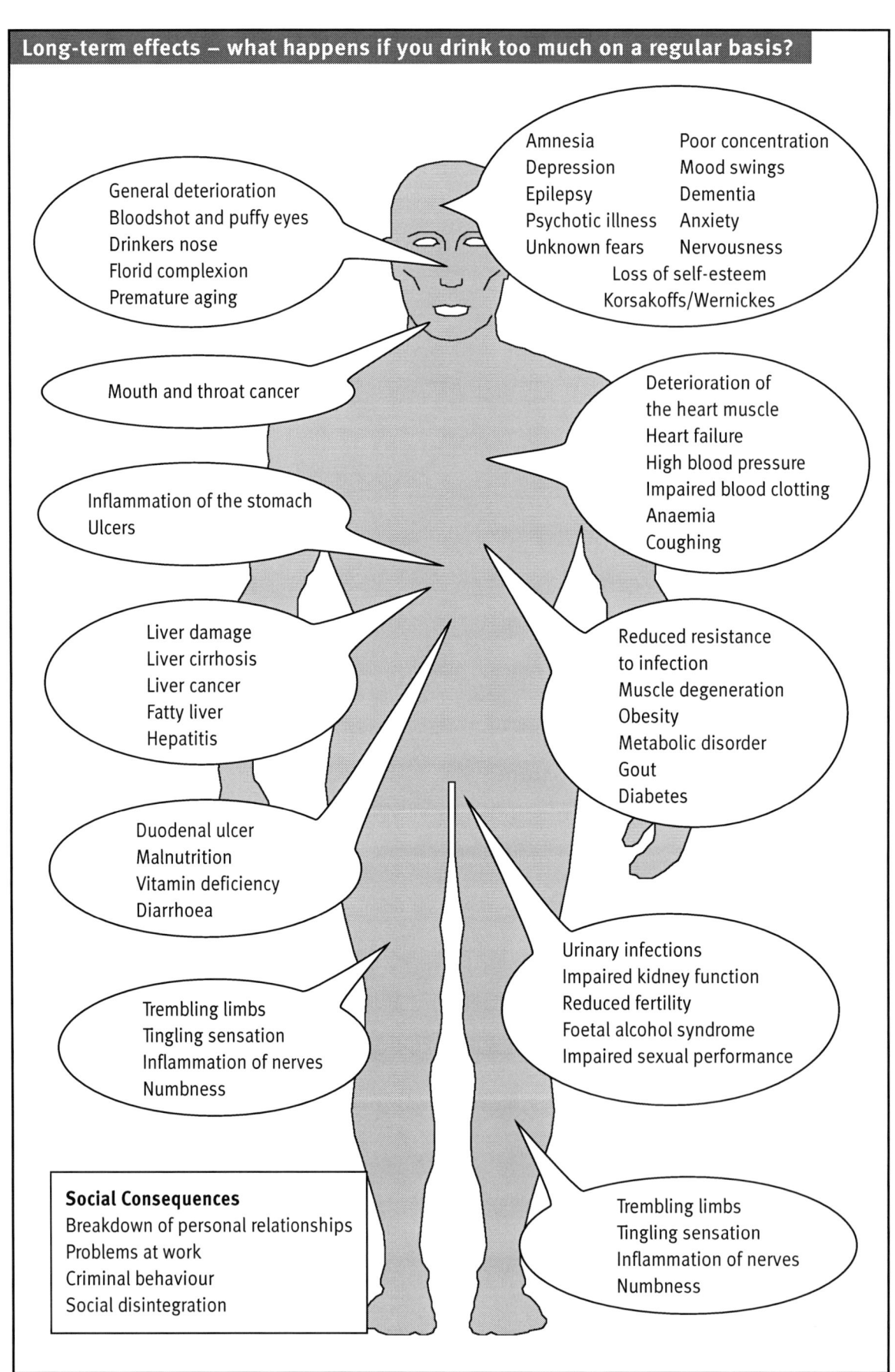

General deterioration
Bloodshot and puffy eyes
Drinkers nose
Florid complexion
Premature aging

Amnesia   Poor concentration
Depression   Mood swings
Epilepsy   Dementia
Psychotic illness   Anxiety
Unknown fears   Nervousness
           Loss of self-esteem
           Korsakoffs/Wernickes

Mouth and throat cancer

Deterioration of
the heart muscle
Heart failure
High blood pressure
Impaired blood clotting
Anaemia
Coughing

Inflammation of the stomach
Ulcers

Liver damage
Liver cirrhosis
Liver cancer
Fatty liver
Hepatitis

Reduced resistance
to infection
Muscle degeneration
Obesity
Metabolic disorder
Gout
Diabetes

Duodenal ulcer
Malnutrition
Vitamin deficiency
Diarrhoea

Urinary infections
Impaired kidney function
Reduced fertility
Foetal alcohol syndrome
Impaired sexual performance

Trembling limbs
Tingling sensation
Inflammation of nerves
Numbness

Social Consequences
Breakdown of personal relationships
Problems at work
Criminal behaviour
Social disintegration

Trembling limbs
Tingling sensation
Inflammation of nerves
Numbness

Alcohol drinking and problems to others

Heavy alcohol drinking in one person often seriously impacts on the lives of others. Many families have become severely affected by one member becoming a problem drinker. Emotional and financial problems often occur in such families. Furthermore, it is estimated that three in ten divorces, four in ten cases of domestic violence, and two in ten cases of child abuse are alcohol related.

Children of problem drinkers can often suffer from emotional and psychological problems. The way in which a young person responds to a parents drinking depends on various factors such as, the young person's personality, strong external support systems and to what extent family life meets the young person's emotional and mental needs. Children tend to follow by example: heavy drinking parents tend to produce children who become problem drinkers. However some children react against their parent's example and drink little themselves.

Often the problem drinker denies or refuses to accept that the root cause is alcohol. This and other social or emotional issues at home will impact on how receptive a young person will be to alcohol education.

Units

A unit is a term used to describe a measure of alcohol. One unit is the amount of alcohol the liver can process in one hour and it contains 10ml of pure alcohol. It is a useful way of counting how much alcohol you are consuming and of seeing how different drinks compare. Alcohol drinks have varying strengths and are measured as a percentage of alcohol by volume (% ABV), which is nowadays marked on the label of drinks. The higher the percentage the stronger the drink will be.

The following drinks in **standard pub measures** each contain **approximately** one unit of alcohol:
- A single measure of spirits
- Half a pint of average strength beer or lager
- A standard glass of wine
- A small glass of sherry

Many pubs, particularly in Scotland, do not use standard measures and therefore units can be difficult to gauge. Most young people tend to drink from bottles or cans, so seeing the units consumed in terms of pub measures is not always appropriate. It is also problematic calculating units if you are drinking from a shared bottle outdoors, as many young people do. For adults, home measures are twice the usual amount in a pub.

You can work out the exact number of units in a drink by multiplying the amount of liquid you are drinking in millilitres (ml) by the percentage of alcohol it contains (%ABV) and dividing it by 1000.

$$\text{Number of units} = \frac{\text{amount of the drink (ml)} \times \text{alcohol percentage (\%ABV)}}{1000}$$

For example: 275ml bottle of Bacardi Breezer (Alcopop) with 5.2 % alcohol content

$$= \frac{275 \times 5.2}{1000} = 1.4 \text{ units}$$

The list below shows the number of units of alcohol in common drinks. Ciders and extra strength lagers can be as much as three times stronger. So half a pint could be as much as 3 units. A general indication of the strength of the main types of drink is as follows:

Drink	Units
1 pint of ordinary strength lager (Heineken, Carling Black label, Fosters)	2
1 pint of strong lager (Stella Artois, Kronenbourg 1664)	3
1 pint of bitter (John Smith's, Boddingtons)	2
1 pint of ordinary strength cider (Dry Blackthorn, Strongbow)	2
1 glass of red or white wine (175ml)	Approx 2
1 standard pub measure of spirits	1
1 bottle of alcopop (Smirnoff Ice, Bacardi Breezer, WKD)	1.5

Sensible drinking levels

The Government report 'Sensible Drinking' (December 1995) shifted the recommended 'safe' drinking levels from a weekly to a daily limit. This was principally to avoid the risk of people interpreting the previously recommended guidance of 21 units for men (14 units for women) as a licence to 'binge'. It makes the point that regular moderate drinking is preferable to drinking large amounts at one time. The report states that regular consumption of the following amounts of alcohol will not 'accrue significant health risk':
- for 'men of all ages', 3-4 units per day.
- for 'women of all ages', 2-3 units per day.

It should however be noted that these figures relate to fully-grown adults and not to young 'under age' drinkers. There is no safe limit for young people because their bodies are smaller than adults and are still maturing so effects of alcohol use will be intensified and generally more damaging. The brain is still developing in young people too.

Binge drinking

There is no commonly-accepted definition for binge-drinking. The Office of National Statistics (ONS) and The Scottish Health Survey uses the criterion of drinking more than twice the recommended daily benchmark on a person's heaviest drinking day as being hazardous and consequently a 'binge'. This would mean more than eight units for a man and more than six units for a female. One in four adults are drinking in this way. This lack of consensus is illustrated by another definition provided by the International Centre for Alcohol Policies, which thereby states that binge drinking is consuming 'ten or more drinks in one session' (based on one drink as a standardised unit of 10ml ethanol).

Binge drinking for young people has been defined as drinking five or more alcoholic drinks in a single session. Of people aged 16-74, 15 per cent of men drank more than 35 units per week and six per cent of women drank more than 21 units per week (Scottish Health Survey, 1998).

Statistics provided for 2001 showed the biggest increase of binge drinking to be amongst the 16-24 age-group. In women, hazardous drinking reached its peak in the age-group 16-19, with just under one third (32 per cent) having a hazardous drinking pattern. In men, the peak was found to be in the 20-24 age group, with just under two thirds (62 per cent) having a hazardous drinking pattern.

Binge drinking has been highlighted as a major concern within the UK in terms of long-term health consequences and immediate behavioural costs, such as sexual health practices.

A study conducted by The Health Education Authority (1998) found that amongst 16-24 year olds:
- 1 in 7 have had unsafe sex.
- 1 in 5 had sex they later regretted.
- 1 in 10 were unable to remember sex the night before.
- 40% agreed they were more likely to have casual sex.

Binge drinking is an important focus for alcohol education to raise awareness of the dangers. Resultant problems such as accidents, injuries, unprotected sex and drink driving are all huge risks for a young person.

Mental health

Alcohol can cause psychological problems and psychological problems can lead to alcohol misuse. Changes in the brain caused by alcohol mimic changes found in depressive disorders and in some cases it is difficult to determine which the initial issue was. Potential psychological problems are:
- depression.
- anxiety.

- amnesia.
- hallucinations.
- psychotic illness (e.g. schizophrenia).
- morbid jealousy.

The life of a problem drinker with anxieties about behaviour and possibly poor work performance all contribute to feelings of depression. In these cases the depression is secondary to the actual drinking problem. Alcohol misuse can also be a symptom of underlying depressive illness for some patients, mostly women. In a lot of cases abstinence can reduce mental health issues in an individual.

Suicide is a very significant risk in patients who have a serious alcohol problem, particularly where this is associated with depression or a tendency for impulsive behaviour. Forty per cent of male and eight per cent of female attempted suicides are chronic problem drinkers, and 15-25 per cent of actual suicides in England and Wales can be associated with alcohol misuse. In the year 2000, 15 per cent of all psychiatric hospital admissions in Scotland had an alcohol-related diagnosis (Scottish Executive, March 2004).

Alcohol is the most widely used substance for 'self medication'. Harmful drinking can arise from some individuals using alcohol as a coping strategy to face social and other anxieties that they would otherwise be unable to do. While most careful users can manage perfectly well, there are regular heavy users that become tolerant and addicted in a way that is hard to break free from. In addition, the alcohol lowers inhibitions and encourages the user to express their inner feelings. If these suppressed emotions are frustration or anger the use of alcohol can lead to aggression or violence.

Women and alcohol

Around 375,000, or 1 in 50 women, in the UK are considered to be very heavy drinkers (Strategy Unit Alcohol Harm Reduction Report, September 2003). A woman who drinks over 35 units per week is considered to be a 'very heavy drinker' and runs the risk of damaging her body more severely and more quickly than a man.

Generally women are affected by alcohol more quickly than men and the effects last longer. This is partly due to the fact that women are generally smaller and lighter than men, but the main reason lies in the fact that women have a higher fat to water ratio than men. Women are genetically predisposed to carry on average 10% more fat, which is needed by the body for childbearing. Consequently less water is available with which to dilute the alcohol intake and the concentration of alcohol in the body will be higher. Women also appear to have lower levels of the enzyme alcohol dehydrogenase (ADH) in their stomachs. This means that it takes longer for the alcohol to begin to be metabolised, detoxified and expelled from the body. In addition, it has been shown that hormone levels can alter the rate at which alcohol is metabolised. Women may be more prone to the effects of alcohol in the pre-menstrual stage of their cycle.

High alcohol use has damaging effects on both the male and female bodies. There are however a number of diseases related to alcohol misuse which are specific to women. These include:
- osteoporosis
- coronary heart disease and strokes
- certain cancers
- intestinal problems
- obesity linked with high blood pressure
- problems relating to childbearing including birth defects

Women also demonstrate a higher propensity to liver disease earlier in their drinking lives than men. It takes less alcohol over a shorter period of time to result in damage in a female body.

Alcohol also takes its toll in childbearing. Women who drink more than three units per day may reduce their ability to conceive and drinking more than one unit per day during the first three months of pregnancy doubles the chances of miscarriage up to the 6th month of pregnancy.

If you are pregnant and you drink alcohol, your baby does too. Alcohol passes across the placenta into the baby's blood stream, in the same way food or oxygen does. Effects of consuming alcohol during pregnancy range from preventing the baby growing properly to 'foetal alcohol syndrome'. The more you drink, the more likely your baby will suffer the effects. Babies born with foetal alcohol syndrome have distinctive features that include an upturned nose, no chin, thin lips, heart, kidney and skeletal defects and birthmarks. Children born to alcohol misusing mothers can, in some instances show no immediate ill effects, however, a number will go on to develop behavioural or cognitive problems. Many perform poorly at school and up to 65 per cent evidence emotional, eating and speech disorders. Damage as a result of alcohol consumption may occur at anytime throughout pregnancy but the foetus is at its most vulnerable at 4-10 weeks gestation. Abstinence is the preferred option; however, reducing consumption at anytime during the pregnancy may benefit the unborn child.

Men and alcohol

Alcohol and men is a developing field of research. The main issues are the prevalence of harmful drinking amongst men, the associated risks and men's awareness of potential problems.

There are a number of key chronic conditions that are significant for men:

- **Liver disease**
  Liver cirrhosis between 1988 and 1999 increased by 94 per cent (1494 to 2904 deaths) compared with a 39 per cent rise in women.

- **Cancer**
  People who drink more than five units per day are more at risk than non-drinkers. Smoking is also a contributor. 80 per cent of cancers could be avoided by abstinence from alcohol and tobacco (Heather et al., 2001).

- **Heart disease and strokes**
  Five to seven per cent of diagnosed cases of hypertension are caused by heavy drinking and is the commonest cause after obesity. Hypertension is approximately doubled in people who drink over six units a day.

- **Gastritis (stomach problems)**
  Condition often associated with prolonged heavy drinking.

- **Osteoporosis (reduced bone mass)**
  Normally associated with women, 50 per cent of male heavy drinkers develop osteoporosis.

- **Sexual problems**
  Prolonged heavy drinking can cause loss of libido and can lead to the shrinking of the testes, reduction in the size of the penis and reduction in sperm count, thereby affecting fertility.

Men's drinking behaviour often has a negative impact on their health, their family's health and the levels of crime and safety in their communities. The media spotlight is rarely directed at men's drinking patterns compared to women and young people; however, men are twice as likely to exceed safe drinking levels of alcohol. One in nine adult men in Britain is dependent on alcohol. Men are three times as likely to be dependent on alcohol as women (National Statistics, 2001).

In general, men are less likely than women to seek medical help or engage in preventative health action. Life expectancy is reduced by excessive alcohol use and is five years less than a man in similar circumstances. More than two thirds (73 per cent) of alcohol related deaths were men. The majority of deaths are in the 45-64 age-group. However, the number of alcohol related deaths in younger men (30-45) has doubled in more recent years.

Patterns of behaviour that make men more vulnerable to harm, include risk taking, such as experimenting with drugs, having unprotected sex, involvement in arguments, injuring themselves or others, having the inability to turn up to work the morning after or driving a car under the influence of alcohol (National Statistics, 2001; Purser, 2001). Excess and problem drinking is higher in the poorest socio-economic groups, particularly among 25-39-year-old men. Male admissions to hospital for combined mental health and alcohol related conditions are more than twice those for women (3,070 male and 1,362 females in 2001). Most of these admissions were for people of middle age, however a notable trend in the last two decades has been the marked increase in young male suicide rates. In 1999 for 15-24-year-old men there were 16 per 100,000 population compared to a rate of 7 per 100,000 in 1971. There is a strong correlation between alcohol use and male suicides.

Drinking patterns

Although drinking is a normal part of socialising in many countries, there are some worrying trends and statistics, arising from data collected in 2002. More women are drinking above recommended limits, under-age drinking is increasing, binge-drinking is becoming more of a problem, alcohol related deaths are increasing, alcohol-related accidents and illnesses are much more apparent. Statistics suggest that these issues are more problematic in Scotland, as demonstrated by the following graph:

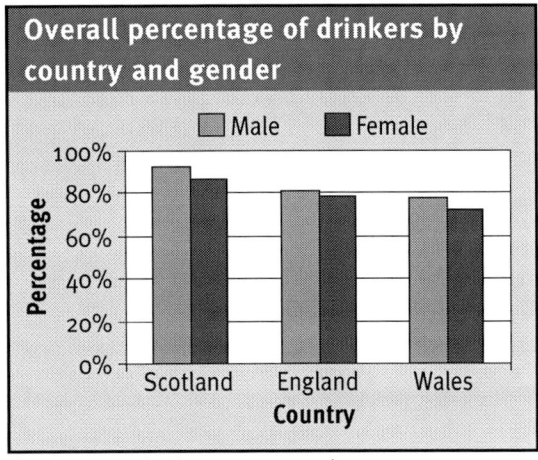

Overall percentage of drinkers by country and gender

(Source: Alcohol Concern, 2001)

Scottish men and women are more likely to have drunk more than twice the recommended daily benchmarks than those in England (General Household Survey, 1998). These statistics are from self reported consumption patterns.

Young people and alcohol

Being able to hold your drink is often seen by young people as a sign of maturity and experience; a rite of passage. The main reasons given by young people for drinking are:

- For the effect (changing mood, coping with stress, feeling happy).
- To be social (to bond with friends, peer pressure, it is socially acceptable).
- To escape (from pressures and problems).
- It is available (it is cheap and easy to get).

Young people may binge-drink, however most will not go on to develop serious problems. Common problems associated with teenage drinking are the effects of severe intoxification and accidents. In addition, there is a link between drinking before sexual activity and unsafe sex. If drunk, a young person is more likely to have sex; to have unprotected sex and to pick up a sexually transmitted infection (STI).

Research suggests a link between young offending and alcohol in that 25 per cent of young prisoners had been drinking when they committed their crime. Alcohol is also implicated in school exclusion statistics, 20 per cent of pupils excluded were under the influence of alcohol at school and 16 per cent of excluded pupils drink every day.

Young people drink mainly cider, beer, lager and wine. The trend towards consumption of alcopops has generally decreased since 1996; however, recent statistics demonstrated an increase in 2000/2001. In 2001 pre-mixed spirits are reported to have been drunk by 30 per cent of 15-16-year-old females. Young people are now consuming stronger drinks such as strong brands of beer, cider and wine as well as vodka.

Amongst the younger adolescents (under 13 years) the most common site of alcohol consumption is in the home, or the home of relatives and friends. As they grow older, young people continue to drink at home, but the usual place of their drinking shifts to parties, then clubs and discos and finally to pubs. Other places where young people commonly drink are public places such as streets and parks.

How much do young people drink?

Mean alcohol consumption (units) of those who had drunk in the last seven days by gender and age: 1996-2002.

Age	Year				
	1996	1998	2000	2001	2002
Boys					
11-13 yrs	7.1	6.2	5.5	5.5	7.2
14 yrs	7.3	12.3	10	10	10.7
15 yrs	12.9	12.9	13.8	13.8	14.3
Total	**9.7**	**11.3**	**10.6**	**10.6**	**11.5**
Girls					
11-13 yrs	4	6.4	4.6	5.7	6.4
14 yrs	8.2	8.1	10.1	9.3	10
15 yrs	8	9.7	11.2	10.7	11.4
Total	**7**	**8.4**	**9.1**	**8.9**	**9.6**
All pupils					
11-13 yrs	5.5	6.3	6.4	5.6	6.8
14 yrs	7.7	9.8	9.8	9.6	10.3
15 yrs	10.4	11.5	12.9	12.3	12.9
Total	**8.4**	**9.9**	**10.4**	**9.8**	**10.5**

How many young people drink?

Percentage of pupils in England who drank last week, by gender and age: 1990-2002.

Age	Year								
	1990	1992	1994	1996	1998	1999	2000	2001	2002
Boys									
11 yrs	8	8	8	7	4	7	5	8	7
12 yrs	9	13	10	12	14	10	11	14	12
13 yrs	17	15	22	27	16	16	18	22	20
14 yrs	32	32	34	37	28	28	34	35	34
15 yrs	42	49	52	50	48	48	52	54	49
Total	**22**	**24**	**26**	**27**	**23**	**22**	**25**	**28**	**25**
Girls									
11 yrs	4	5	4	6	2	4	5	4	4
12 yrs	6	7	9	9	6	8	9	11	9
13 yrs	19	11	16	22	14	17	19	22	21
14 yrs	32	24	26	35	29	28	31	35	34
15 yrs	39	40	48	55	40	41	46	50	45
Total	**20**	**17**	**22**	**26**	**18**	**20**	**23**	**25**	**25**
All pupils									
11 yrs	6	6	6	7	3	6	5	6	5
12 yrs	8	10	9	11	10	9	10	12	11
13 yrs	18	13	19	24	15	16	19	22	20
14 yrs	32	29	30	36	29	28	32	35	34
15 yrs	40	45	50	53	44	45	49	52	47
Total	**21**	**21**	**24**	**27**	**21**	**21**	**24**	**26**	**24**

(Source IAS, 2003)

Hammered
Young people and alcohol

Statistics are reporting that not only are more children and young people drinking, but they are drinking more. The proportion of young people 12-15 in Scotland, who had had an alcoholic drink in the previous week rose from 14 per cent in 1990 to 21 per cent in 2000. Figures show those that had been drunk within the last seven days had increased their average weekly consumption from 8.4 units to 11.1 units. Four out of ten children aged 15 had had a drink in the last week. More girls are drinking at least once a week. In 1990, boys were more likely to have had a drink in the previous week compared with girls (16% compared with 12%), this gap has been virtually closed in 2000 (21% compared with 20%). (Scottish Executive, March 2004). See the graph below.

Drinking is more common amongst older adolescents (15-16-years-old) with almost 33 per cent drinking at least once a week. Statistics also show that by the age of 13 young people who drink outnumber the young people who don't drink. The UK figures for alcohol consumption were some of the highest amongst a European study of drinking among 15-16-year-olds.

In 2000, there were 1,428 emergency admissions in the UK of young people aged 10-19 with a diagnosed intoxification. Admissions were highest (1036) in the 15-19-year-age group.

In 1999/2000 there were 1,260 referrals to the Childrens Hearing System in Scotland on misuse of alcohol or drugs. This represents 2 per cent of all referrals to the Hearing System referrals (Scottish Children Reporter Administration, Care and Justice for All Children Annual Report, 1999-2000, SCRA).

Black Minority Ethnic communities and alcohol issues

The quality of data in the area of alcohol use and Black Minority Ethnic (BME) communities is patchy. Most research has focussed on the Afro-Caribbean and various South Asian communities living in the UK. These communities have been the most visible migrant groups of the last 40 years. They have experienced a high degree of racism and discrimination which contributes to social and economic disadvantage. These factors are closely associated with an increased risk of alcohol misuse and

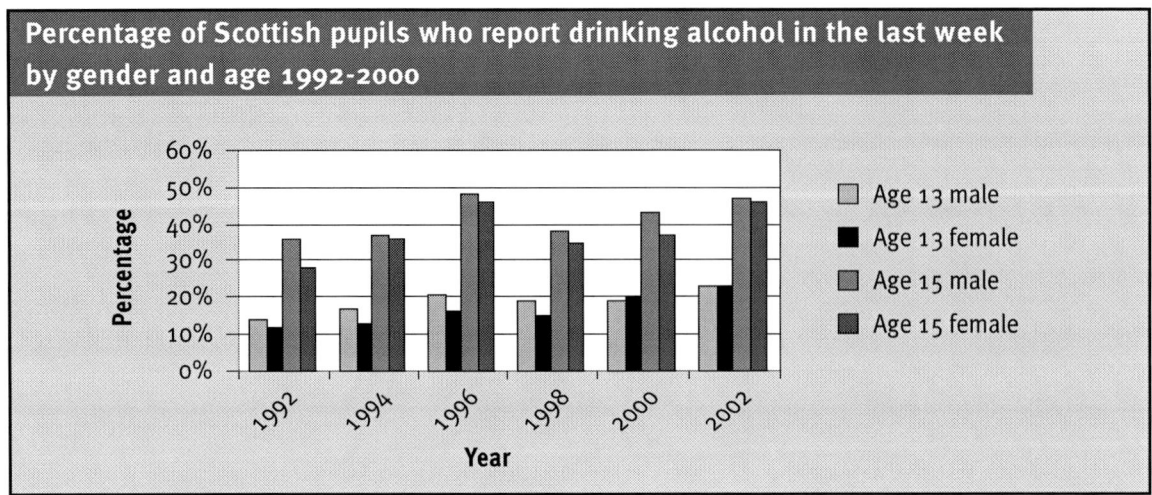

Percentage of Scottish pupils who report drinking alcohol in the last week by gender and age 1992-2000

Source: Scottish Schools Adolescent Lifestyle and Substance Use Survey, 2002 undertaken by the Child and Adolescent Health Research Unit commissioned by the ISD Scotland.

Hammered
Young people and alcohol

therefore provide good reason for information and prevention work with BME groups.

The 1999 report *Health of minority ethnic groups* provides a current national set of data on drinking amongst ethnic groups, based on self-report questionnaire interviews. Findings indicate that men and women from BME groups are less likely to drink alcohol than the general population. Overall they drink smaller quantities and drink patterns are less frequent than the general population. Similarly among ethnic groups higher proportions of women are non-drinkers in comparison with their male counterparts.

Percentage of non drinkers (male and female BME communities)		
	Men	**Women**
General population	7	12
Irish	5	10
Black Caribbean	13	18
Chinese	30	41
Indian	33	64
Pakistani	91	No figures available
Bangladeshi	96	99

Research shows that although the overall picture is of lower levels of consumption amongst most minority groups, a significant percentage of the Indian and Black Caribbean communities exceed weekly limits. Among those who do drink, *both* men and women are exceeding the daily limits.

Patterns of drinking differ also in younger BME people. Among 11 to 15-year-old adolescents from ethnic groups only 18 per cent of Asian and 44 per cent of black young people said they had tried alcohol compared to 66 per cent of young people. 82 per cent of young people in Asian communities and 56 per cent from Black communities report abstinence in contrast to 33 per cent from Caucasian groups.

Gathering information from BME groups can be problematic, more so where cultural and religious influences impact on responses. For instance in some communities it might be unacceptable to admit to alcohol use, therefore no accurate picture can be obtained. In addition, traditional methods of gathering data on the general population do not provide specific information on ethnic sub-groups. However, surveys focusing on individual communities are beginning to show clear differences in the drinking patterns of Sikh and Hindu male populations.

Alcohol-related social consequences

Alcohol use is implicated as a factor in a number of negative social issues, as demonstrated by the statistics outlined below.

Alcohol-related deaths 1990-1999		
Year	**Number of Deaths**	
	Scotland	**England & Wales**
1990	640	3,594
1991	620	3,631
1992	700	3,553
1993	790	3,546
1994	860	3,821
1995	960	4,231
1996	1,160	4,455
1997	1,390	4,933
1998	1,485	5,272
1999	1,600	5,473
2000	1,694	5,543
2001	1,771	6,020
2002	1,957	6,100

(Source: GRO)

Hammered
Young people and alcohol

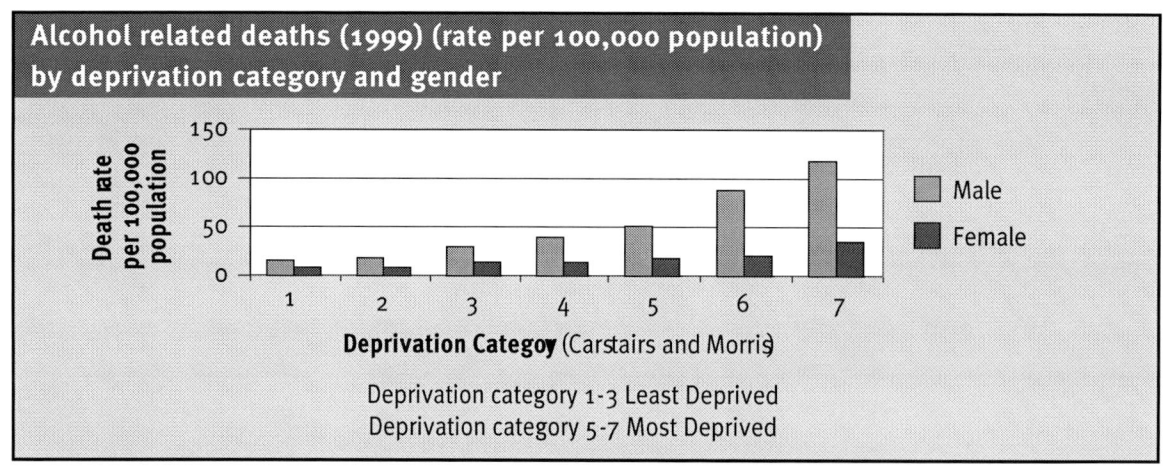

Alcohol related deaths (1999) (rate per 100,000 population) by deprivation category and gender

Death rate per 100,000 population

Deprivation Category (Carstairs and Morris)

Deprivation category 1-3 Least Deprived
Deprivation category 5-7 Most Deprived

Source: GRO

Year	England and Wales	Scotland	Northern Ireland	Total	Rate per 10,000
1964	73,299	10,778	1,731	85,808	15.9
1984*	81,669	6,618	322	88,609	15.7
1994	57,890	1,429	94	59,413	10.2
1999	49,020	478	100	49,598	8.3
2000	45,234	434	75	45,768	7.8
2001	42,885	371	62	43,356	7.4

Arrests for 'drunk and disorderly' behaviour in the UK

(Source IAS, 2003)

*since 1984 figures for England and Wales, and Scotland have included cautions and convictions.

People living in the most deprived areas are seven times more likely to be admitted to an acute hospital with an alcohol related diagnosis. Hospital inpatient rates with an alcohol diagnosis are seven times higher in Deprivation Category 7 than Deprivation Category 1.

Crime

Although the figures in the table above appear to show a reduction in drunk and disorderly behaviour, in reality police practices have changed since the mid 1980s. Individuals tend not to be charged with drunkenness alone, police officers preferring to restrict arrests and cautions to more serious offences.

Violent crime

The Scottish Crime Survey 2000 stated that 72 per cent of those victims of violent crime reported the assailant was under the influence of alcohol (Scottish Crime Survey, 2000). A similar definition is used for the figures in the table below for UK wide crimes:

Estimated number of incidents of alcohol-related violence UK in 1999	
Alcohol related	**Best estimate**
Stranger assault	450,000
Acquaintance assault	410,000
Domestic assault	320,000
Mugging	66,000
All violence	**1,246,000**

(Source IAS, 2003)

Hammered
Young people and alcohol

Homicides

Within the year 2000, 128 people were accused of homicide. Of the 88 for whom the drink status was known, 61 per cent were drunk. 67 per cent of accused persons over 30 years old were most often drunk. (Homicide in Scotland, 2000; Scottish Executive, 2001). No similar statistics are available from the Home Office for figures in England and Wales.

Drink driving

Roadside screening breath tests 1996-2000			
Year		**England and Wales**	**Scotland**
1996	Number of tests Positive/refused % of total tests	781,000 101,000 13	17,353 577 3.3
1997	Number of tests Positive/refused % of total tests	800,000 104,000 13	18,244 587 3.2
1999	Number of tests Positive/refused % of total tests	764,000 94,000 12	16,631 512 3.1
2000	Number Positive/refused % of total tests	715,000 95,000 13	15,933 526 3.3

Figures are complied from IAS (2003) and Scottish Executive (2001).

Drink-driving offences recorded by the police in 2000			
Nearly 90% per cent of drink driving offences are committed by men			
	England and Wales	**Scotland**	**Total**
2000	76,746	10,712	87,458

*excludes causing death by driving under the influence of drink.
Figures are complied from IAS (2003) and Scottish Executive (2001).

Blood alcohol levels in fatalities aged 16 and over: GB: 2001								
Percentage over blood alcohol levels (mg/100ml)							**Percentage over 80mg/100ml**	
	9	50	80	100	150	200	22.00-03.59 hours	04.00-21.59 hours
Motor cycle riders	22	12	10	10	6	4	48	7
Other vehicle drivers	22	24	22	20	15	10	53	14
Passengers	46	33	30	26	16	11	48	18
Pedestrians	50	43	40	38	30	22	71	25
Cyclists	22	14	12	12	8	6	–	8

IAS, 2003

Hammered
Young people and alcohol

The alcohol industry

Although alcohol is a powerful drug, and implicated in a number of negative health and social consequences, it is legal and widely available. Alcohol is big business. In 1999/2000 alone, the UK Government raised almost £11.5 billion in revenue from alcohol. In 2001 the alcohol industry spent £181.3 million pounds on advertising compared to the £75.9 million spent advertising soft drinks. The largest proportion was spent on beer at £42.7 million, £18.1 million on spirits and £8.3 million on wine (IAS, 2003).

The advertising of alcohol is a contentious issue which provokes much debate between the drinks industry and those with public health concerns. Advertising condones the use of a potentially harmful drug, encourages consumption and aims to attract 'new users'. In its defence the alcohol industry argues that there is no evidence supporting a link between excessive consumption or alcohol related harm and alcohol advertising. Codes of Practice governing alcohol advertising do exist and are designed to restrict promotion to under 18s, excessive consumption and risky behaviour. Self-regulation by the industry is encouraged but it is debatable how much support it has within the alcohol trade. The significant role held by alcohol consumption in our society contributes to the perpetuation and acceptability of advertising. It is unlikely that there will be a reduction in advertising when the industry generates such enormous revenue.

Alcohol and the law

Licensed premises
Laws that restrict the use of alcohol by young people are specifically related to the selling and consumption of alcohol on licensed premises:

- **Under 14 years of age** – young people are not allowed in the bar of licensed premises, but are allowed on premises with a 'refreshment licence' if accompanied by an adult (over 21) before 8pm. (A refreshment licence is when alcohol is sold only with food and there is no bar).
- **From 16 years of age** – young people are allowed to buy beer, wine, cider, port or perry with a meal, as long as the meal is served in a part of the premises, which is exclusively for the serving of food.
- **From 18 years of age** – young people can work in the bar of a licensed establishment; buy alcohol in a bar and from an off licence.
- It is illegal for anyone under the age of 18 years of age, to buy, or be bought alcohol in a pub or from an off licence. Anyone buying alcohol in a bar for someone under 18 years of age is breaking the law.

Out-with licensed premises
The only law, which restricts the drinking of alcohol by young people, relates to children under five years of age. It is an offence to give alcohol to a child under five years of age except under medical supervision or in an emergency.

Otherwise, it is legal for anyone to drink alcohol as long as it is consumed away from licensed premises. Some towns do however have by-laws, which restrict drinking in certain public places. It is not therefore, in itself, an offence for young people to drink outwith licensed premises e.g. in the park, outside the youth club, but it is highly likely that the law has been broken if they have bought their carry-out

themselves or have got somebody else to do it for them. Anybody who buys alcohol for under 18s or who sells it to someone who is buying it for under 18s is committing an offence.

The police cannot arrest young people for drinking outwith licensed premises but may get involved if a young person is drunk and disorderly or committing a breach of the peace. If there is enough evidence that the young person (under 18 years) has bought the alcohol they have consumed from a particular licensed establishment, the licensee and/or staff and the young person can be charged.

The above is meant only as a general guideline to the Licensing Act. Your local police headquarters licensing department will be able to assist with any specific enquiries.

Drinking and driving

Current legal limits for alcohol levels are 80 milligrams of alcohol per 100 millilitres of blood or 107 mg/100ml in urine or 35 micrograms of alcohol in 100 millilitres of breath. In other European countries this limit is lower at 50mg/100ml of blood. Suggested drinking limits to ensure you remain within legally acceptable limits cannot be given (except abstinence!) because every individual will be different. The rate of absorption will depend on, amongst other things, your size, gender, and how much food you ate before you drank. Realistically there is no safe amount that can be drunk before driving or operating machinery, as any quantity of alcohol will affect the body, impairing judgement and slowing reaction times. Some people will have reached this limit, after drinking as little as three units.

However, even if a driver is below the legal limit, it is likely that their driving performance will be affected even by moderate amounts of alcohol. Their reaction time will be slower and their judgement affected.

Much has been invested in anti-drink driving campaigns and police authorities continue to devote time to spot checking drivers, particularly around the festive period, however the number of positive breath tests continue to rise. Research prepared for the Scottish Executive showed that 30 per cent of drivers admitted getting behind the wheel while possibly over the limit, compared with 22 per cent in a similar survey conducted in 2001.

Alcohol education work with young people should emphasise the dangers of mixing alcohol and driving. Whether they would be driving themselves or a passenger of someone who is over the limit they should be aware of what the health, legal and possibly career consequences could be.

Cultural influence

From the earliest record, use of alcohol has been part of cultures worldwide. It has been used for both social activity and religious purposes. Seen as part of our way of life, it is hard to envisage the daily practices of socialising, celebrating and even mourning without the use of alcohol. In a significant number of societies today alcohol also plays a central role in transitional rituals, both major life-cycle events and minor everyday transitions. For young people, consuming alcohol is a sign of maturity and everyday adults drink to mark the transition from work to play. Alcohol is also associated with celebration and drinking in

all cultures can be regarded as an essential element of festivity. Cultures in Britain, United States, Scandinavia and Australia all use alcohol for celebrations where the event often becomes an excuse for excess.

In Britain 'drinking' used to lie more in the domain of men. Today women are just as involved in the lad or ladette binge drinking culture too. Cultures where drinking is associated with recreation which leads to irresponsibility, tend to have higher levels of alcohol related problems. Studies show that the overall alcohol consumption of the British is lower than in continental Europe, Australia and New Zealand, but that we indulge in binge drinking rather than steady consumption as in other countries. There is enormous cross-cultural variation in the way people behave when they drink. In some societies (such as Britain, Scandinavia, United States and Australia) alcohol is associated with violent and anti-social behaviour, while other (such as Mediterranean and some South American cultures) drinking behaviour is largely peaceful and harmonious.

Helping agencies

There are a number of agencies at both local and national level providing expert and professional advice on alcohol and alcohol related problems. Most areas will have a local Council on Alcohol (see under 'Counselling and Advice' in the Yellow Pages), which will provide information, education and counselling services.

- **AL-ANON Family Groups UK and Eire**
  www.al-anonuk.org.uk
  61 Great Dover Street, London SE1 4YF
  Tel: 020 7403 0888 – 24 hr helpline
  Fax: 020 7378 9910

Al-Anon's aim is to help families and friends of alcoholics recover from the effects of living with the problem drinking of a relative or friend.

- **Alcoholics Anonymous**
  PO Box 1, Stonebow House, Stonebow, York YO1 7NJ
  Tel: 01904 644026
  Helpline: 0845 769 7555
  Web: http://www.alcoholics-anonymous.org.uk

- **Alcohol Concern**
  www.alcoholconcern.org.uk
  Waterbridge House, 32-36 Loman Street, London, SE1 0EE
  Alcohol Concern is the national agency on alcohol misuse. This site contains information about the work of Alcohol Concern, copies of their press releases, fact sheets and other publications.

- **Alcohol Focus Scotland**
  Alcohol Focus Scotland (formerly The Scottish Council on Alcohol) offers a comprehensive range of services at national level.
  166 Buchanan Street Glasgow G1 2LW
  Tel: 0141 333 9677

- **Down Your Drink**
  www.downyourdrink.org.uk
  An online programme for people who are worried about their drinking. The online course is in six weekly parts, based on practical methods to reduce drinking as recommended by leaders in the alcohol, education and treatment field. It takes less than an hour a week online, for 6 weeks, to complete the course, during which time you are taught how to become a "Thinker Drinker" and develop safer drinking habits.

- **Drinkline The National Alcohol Helpline**
  Tel: 0800 917 8282

- **Drinkwise**
  Alcohol Focus Scotland,
  2nd Floor, 166 Buchanan Street,
  Glasgow, G1 2LW.
  Tel: 0141 572 6700
  Web: www.drinkwise.co.uk
  The aim behind the Drinkwise campaign is basically to promote the re-appraisal of personal drinking behaviour. It promotes personal responsibility for drinking and its consequences.

- **Health Development Agency**
  Holborn Gate 330 High Holborn London WC1V 7BA
  Tel: 0 20 7430 0850
  Web: www.hda-online.org.uk

- **Health Scotland**
  www.hebs.scot.nhs.uk
  Woodburn House, Canaan Lane,
  Edinburgh EH10 4SG
  Tel: 0131 536 5500
  Fax: 0131 536 5501
  The public side of this site contains a wide range of information and statistics on a variety of health-related topics.

- **Institute of Alcohol Studies**
  www.ias.org.uk
  1 The Quay, St Ives, Cambridgeshire PE17 4AR
  Tel: 01480 466766
  Fax: 01480 497583
  The Institute of Alcohol Studies (IAS) is an educational body with the basic aims of increasing knowledge of alcohol and the social and health consequences of its misuse.

- **National Association of Children of Alcoholics**
  Helpline: 0800 289061
  Web: www.nacoa.org.uk

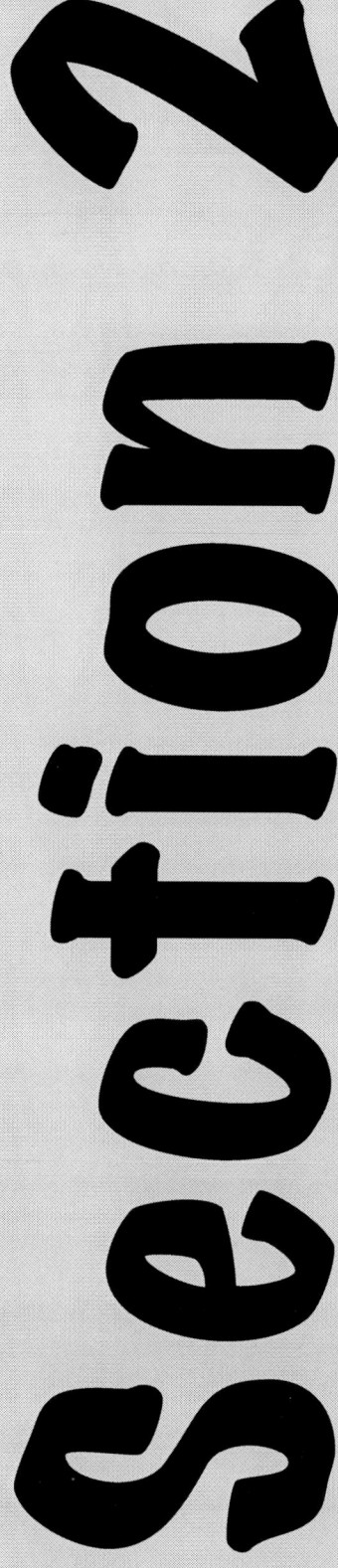

Section 2

Hammered
Young people and alcohol

Developing and Running an Alcohol Education Programme

If you work with young people you have probably undertaken some sort of structured intervention work with them already. Running an alcohol education programme is no different. You do need to know facts about alcohol, but you will already have plenty of knowledge, skills and experience of working with young people. Everyday you connect with them. You listen and respond to their needs, choosing the most appropriate way to deal with a whole range of issues as they arise. Alcohol education is just another issue or topic to be tackled.

Getting started

Before you can plan an alcohol education programme (or any programme for that matter) you must identify:
- Why you are doing it (your aim).
- What you want the young people to get out of it.
- What are the needs of the young people taking part?
- What resources are available (staff, funds, venue, and materials).
- What the timescale is.

Answers to these points will help inform not only your objectives but the methods too.

Be honest about what is available to you and realistic about what you can achieve. If, for example, your aim is to *'stop young people drinking alcohol'*, the likelihood is that this is an impossible task. On the other hand, if you aim to *'increase young*

people's awareness of alcohol and alcohol issues' to allow them to make informed choices, this is infinitely more achievable.

If this is the aim then your objectives might look something like this:
- To provide an understanding of alcohol and society.
- To raise awareness of alcohol and its physical, emotional and social effects.
- To explore young people's understanding of alcohol related issues.
- To examine and challenge the views of young people.

A number of practicalities will impact on how you meet your objectives and these are discussed below.

Group structure

How many young people are you working with? Ideally groups of 8-10 individuals are the best size for generating discussion. Big enough to bring a number of thoughts, ideas and experiences, but small enough not to be too threatening for the more self-conscious young person. The bigger the group the less individual interaction you will have with each person. If you have a large number of young people you wish to work with you could take a small group at a time or, if you have help, start with a large group input (general information, quizzes, for example) and split into smaller groups for more intimate or challenging exercises.

You should also think about gender issues. Single gender groups can offer space where

specific issues, such as safe sex, might be discussed more openly and honestly than in a mixed group. Then again, a mixed group might offer the opportunity to gain insight into 'what it's like for the opposite sex'. It will depend on the focus of the work and what you want to achieve.

Age is yet another consideration. A group with participants who span a wide age range is more difficult to work with. Eleven-year-olds will have different needs and experiences than seventeen-year-olds. However, yet again it may hold some unusual learning opportunities.

The life stage of the group will also have a bearing on what work you will be able to do with your group. Established groups (those who have progressed through the forming, storming and norming phases) will be able to tackle 'riskier' subjects. More intimate methods (e.g. role play) will also be more acceptable to them. Choose your tasks wisely, so as not to dissuade your young people from taking part.

Sessions

This will depend very much on your timescale and resource availability. Your young people may only be available to you for one to two hours (as in street work for example) or you may be able to run something two nights a week for six weeks. Ideally we would be able to have enough time and resources to deliver an in-depth programme to meet all the needs of the young people. In the real world we are very much constrained. At Fast Forward we believe that to deliver effective education and prevention work we need at least two hours, preferably a lot more. Contact that is one-off and is for less than an hour, will probably only allow for basic information

giving (however, knowing someone is available to speak to if necessary can be an enormously beneficial resource to young people and cannot be underrated).

In answer to the question 'how many sessions?' – make the programme as long as realistically possible. For example four, two hour sessions would enable you to spend time on information, attitudes and pertinent issues. Some groups may find it difficult to engage with an extended programme initially so it is worthwhile viewing each session as a stand alone input which includes a variety of exercises tackling the different issues you would like to cover.

If you can undertake an extended piece of work, running it as a block programme tends to be more successful. It allows themes and ideas to develop and can be a good way of generating a young person led project. For example, developing an information leaflet or video about local alcohol issues.

One-off sessions are more appropriate to groups that workers know less well, or which do not have a regular stable membership e.g. a group that meets within a larger youth club on an ad-hoc basis.

The programme

The format, content and intended outcomes of each programme will differ for each group. You may run a programme several times but on each occasion participants, group dynamics and individual needs will change. How you choose to structure your work will also be influenced by experience of staff, numbers of staff available, knowledge of the group and the level at which the group is functioning.

Programmes or just a one off input can be structured to include a number of different elements, for example:

- Finding out what participants want from the session.
- Finding out existing alcohol knowledge and their perception of alcohol use.
- Information giving.
- Challenging and exploring attitudes.
- Problem solving.

If time is short you will need to decide which are the most important topics for the group you are working with. If possible, ask the young people which areas they would like to cover and try to include them.

Whichever way you decide the content, make sure your input is balanced. For example, spend time on alcohol information and facts but also look at making choices, so they have an idea of how to put the things they have learnt into practice.

An example programme is given below:

Alcohol awareness programme for young people

Learning outcomes

- Challenge perceptions
- Identify why people drink
- Understanding the effects alcohol has on the body
- Understanding safe units and binge drinking

Outline of session

Exercise/Activity	Format	Aim
Welcome and introductions	Large group.	Introduce group and trainers. Outline of session and learning outcomes.
Name game	Large group.	Relax group and to set the scene.
One for the road	Large group.	To identify positive and negative associations with alcohol and reasons why people like to drink.
Alcohol awareness quiz	Individuals, pairs or in teams as appropriate. Feedback in large group.	To provide young people with facts about alcohol in an informative and fun way.
Body bits	Small groups. Poster exercise using a 'flip chart body' and coloured pens.	Establish the physical effects of alcohol on the body and social consequences.
The knowledge	Large group. Unit quiz.	Looking at safe drinking guidelines. Examining the differences between men and women. Examining financial implications.
Case studies	Small groups. Feedback in large group.	Problem solving, tackling possible scenarios they may come across and outline harm reduction strategies.
Question and answers evaluation Hand-out publications	Large group.	To discover the outcomes for your young people.

Hammered
Young people and alcohol

Topics

The issues you decide to cover in your programme could include some of the following:

- The effects of alcohol, both the social and health consequences.
- What is a unit of alcohol and what this means to a young person's drinking.
- Reasons why people drink. This could be gender specific depending on the group you are working with.
- Safer drinking – can drinking be safe, is it different for men and women?
- Differences between male and female alcohol consumption, reasons for and effects of.
- Dealing with emergencies linked to alcohol use and abuse.
- Mixing drugs and alcohol.
- Alcohol and the law.
- Sources of help and advice.
- Looking at and challenging stereotypical behaviour. Again, this could be gender specific.
- Cultural attitudes and expectations of alcohol use.
- Political and economic aspects of alcohol.
- Peer pressure.
- Making personal choices.
- Tackling difficult situations.

This is not an exhaustive list and any issues generated from within the group should be considered as possible topics for closer scrutiny.

You may find your young people are more interested in the short-term more personal effects of alcohol e.g. weight gain, skin changes etc. to begin with. The use of fun, interactive exercises with no pressure or lectures will encourage them to want to find out more about other aspects of alcohol use, misuse and culture.

Using exercises

There are a number of exercise examples in the next chapter. They are grouped into sections according to their purpose and by choosing an exercise from each section you can create a balanced alcohol education programme.

It is a good idea to build up your own store of appropriate exercises that will help you deliver the message or information you want to get across. You will have come across other types of exercises that work really well with young people; with a little adaptation you can give them an alcohol focus and 'hey-presto!' you have a new alcohol exercise to add to your collection.

When designing new exercises it is useful to think about:

- What makes you hang on to information, what makes you believe it, accept it and use it?
- When retaining information wasn't so successful, what made it difficult to take in, accept and use it?

Also think about:

- Who is it for?
- What is its purpose or message?
- What do you want the participants to get out of it?
- What methods are you going to use?
- How much time does the exercise need?
- What resources do you need?
- How will it run? (in a small group, individually, pairs, etc.)

Most new exercises are based on others that have gone before, they just need to be made young person friendly. Young people are excellent at knowing what will work for young people, so involve them where you can. At the very least consult with them to

find out what's in and what's out; the latest gadgets, fads, fashions and crazes. Better still, get them involved in creating their own new exercises. This, in turn can lead to a young person led project in its own right!

Role models

From birth we are all, consciously or unconsciously, influenced by role models. As we are growing up we often admire someone or the things they do. We may adjust our attitudes, decisions and actions to match that of our role model.

It is thought that role models impact upon young people's lives. For example, the attitudes and choices (both positive and negative) of celebrities can very often become the actions and behaviours of the younger generation. Unfortunately even if the behaviour is detrimental and the consequences severe, young people are often proud of themselves for emulating their chosen role model.

Some role models are not as obvious as celebrities or parents and carers. Any adult who has more than passing contact with young people is likely to impact upon their lives. The relationship built between young people attending a youth club and the worker can be significant enough to influence behaviour. Young people are observant, critical, trusting, gullible and cynical all at once. As a worker your actions, in and out of the club, will not go unnoticed and in turn undoubtedly reinforce behaviours, positive or negative. It is worth trying to see 'you' as they see you and identify the obvious or hidden messages you might be giving to the groups you work with. At the very least, be aware of the extent of the impact you have and make positive use of it in your work.

Evaluation

After you have delivered your alcohol education programme or tried out an exercise, it is essential to evaluate it. Evaluation can be simple or complicated. The subject itself is too big to go into here, but it should not be ignored.

Knowing whether an education programme or exercise was successful is important. If it worked you can use it again, if it didn't you need to understand why and if need be take it back to the drawing board. At the very least, ask the young people how it was for them. Use post-it notes or a graffiti wall for simple pictures, one word or one sentence thoughts. Questionnaires are another option; they can give more information but take more time and are more difficult to fill out.

There are many publications available providing information on the subject of evaluation. Do not be daunted by it and make sure you sort out your evaluation process and methods before you start your alcohol education programme.

Work with other groups

Detached work
Detached work offers individual advice, support and risk reduction interventions through engaging with young people in a street-work setting. It has been found to have an important role in communicating with hard to reach audiences by taking services 'to them' rather than expecting them to come to the service.

Detached work, by its nature has to be very flexible and might seem, at first glance, to be incompatible with the development of alcohol education programmes. However, a good understanding of the principles of detached work will provide the foundation for alcohol or any other education focus. Realistically you will not be able to run comprehensive programmes. More often than not you might only have five to ten minutes with a young person or group and you will need to be skilful enough to effectively engage them and hold their interest to successfully impart any useful information. There are a number of key points which will help to make the detached alcohol education more effective. See the table below,

It is also beneficial to use exercises which build upon motivation, participation and engagement as part of any education work.

Once the young people feel 'safe' with you and one another they will generate their own ideas allowing you to build and expand your work.

Engaging with young people through detached work can be erratic and inconsistent. However, it does offer a valuable process through which to engage those young people who would otherwise have no contact with services and enables the passing on of positive health information. More information about setting up and delivering detached youth work can be found in the publication 'Thinking on Your Feet' by The Prince's Trust-Scotland, see address below in the 'further support' section.

Key points	Purpose
Be opportunistic	You never know when the opportunity will arise. Make use of the young people that are around and what they offer you.
Be flexible	Be prepared to change what you planned or what you are doing, even while you are doing it!
Know your stuff	Learn your subject well enough for you to feel comfortable talking 'off the cuff', so you can respond fully to any alcohol issues or questions that may arise.
Be young person led	Let the young people bring up their thoughts, issues and concerns. They will listen to you for longer if you do. You can then tease things out, expand and explore.
Have a variety of quick exercises up your sleeve	You never know when the opportunity will come up to do a bit more than passing on information. A passing comment might lead to more in depth exploration if there is a quick game or quiz that illustrates the issue.
Carry young person friendly leaflets	You might not have time to enter into a discussion, but an eye catching, entertaining leaflet might be read later by the young person.

Hammered
Young people and alcohol

Adult groups

You will work with a variety of groups for many different reasons and you might find yourself being asked to give an alcohol input to an adult group. To put an alcohol education programme together for adults, such as parents, it will be necessary to go through the same thought process suggested above, choosing the most appropriate topics and exercises. Most adults feel they need a lot of factual information. In our experience, greater benefit is found in challenging attitudes and giving assistance to tackle any issues that they may face. Factual knowledge is important, but confidence in their own abilities to support young people is more productive and better for the young person in the long run. You will need to decide the most appropriate balance for your input.

If you do find yourself working with adults be aware that:

- They tend to be more formal and reserved than young people.
- They might use different language e.g. not 'street slang'.
- They may view alcohol as 'safe' (from media coverage or ignorance).
- They may hold hypocritical views of drug and alcohol use.
- They will have their own experiences with alcohol.
- They may be less willing to discuss personal experiences and opinions.
- They might expect to be 'talked to' rather than actively participate.

Working with parents, as well as the young people themselves offers great benefits for alcohol education work. Done well, it helps parents understand a young person's perspective, challenges stereotypes, allays fears and begins to break down communication barriers which often exist around this subject.

Black minority ethnic groups

Alcohol use in Black Minority Ethnic (BME) communities tends to be less apparent than in White communities and there is a danger that what may often be hidden leads to the assumption that it is not an issue. Although certain BME groups place restrictions on the use of alcohol for religious or cultural reasons, complex patterns of alcohol use within these communities still exist. Alcohol use exposes members of these communities to the risk of a whole range of problems both for themselves and for their relatives and friends. Problems which are compounded in many cases by a community culture which discourages open discussion of alcohol issues and as a result reduces opportunities to deal with those issues. It is thought that BME communities are reluctant to tackle alcohol issues for fear of aggravating the stigma they already feel as members of marginalised groups (Fast Forward, 2004).

A crucial element in creating meaningful alcohol education work is the development of strong, trusting relationships with key community representatives. The activities of BME community groups are dictated by its members and it is essential that these influential representatives support and endorse your work. Making inroads can be a lengthy process taking many months or perhaps even years to generate the opportunity for alcohol education work. Begin by contacting local BME community organisations for advice and ideas of how to take your work forward. It is important that you understand the issues and culture relevant to the group you wish to work with. Ask them what they need and do not make assumptions or use a 'top down approach'.

Further support

The Fast Forward team are available for support, advice or suggestions for the development of any health education programme with young people or adults. Please do not hesitate to get in touch, you can reach us at:

- **Fast Forward Positive Lifestyles Ltd**
  4 Bernard Street Edinburgh EH6 6PP
  Tel: 0131 554 4300
  Fax: 0131 554 4330

Below are a number of additional contacts for further support in creating alcohol education programmes or working with other groups:

- **FRANK**
  Home Office Communications
  Room 239 50 Queen Anne's Gate
  London SW1H 9AT
  Tel: 0800 77 66 00
  Web: www.talktofrank.com
  An interactive website, government funded, for support with substance issues. Can offer advice on programme and project development and also has good information resources on Black Minority Ethnic issues and work.

- **The Prince's Trust – Scotland**
  7th Floor, Fleming house 134 Renfrew Street Glasgow G3 6ST
  Tel: 0141 331 0212.
  Web: www.princes-trust.org.uk
  An organisation working with young people to 'overcome barriers and get their lives working'. Has produced a comprehensive information package and guide to detached and outreach work.

- **National Youth Agency**
  17-23 Albion Street Leicester LE1 6GD
  Tel: 0116 285 3792
  Web: www.nya.org.uk
  A national organisation supporting and promoting youth work. Can offer insight to detached work.

- **www.refugeecouncil.org.uk**
  The largest organisation in the UK working with asylum seekers and refugees.

Hammered
Young people and alcohol

Section 3

Hammered
Young people and alcohol

Exercises and photocopiable resources

The exercises in this chapter are grouped into sections according to their purpose:

- Icebreaking.
- Passing on information.
- Challenging attitudes.
- Tackling situations.

Picking an exercise from each section can create a balanced programme.

Icebreaking

Icebreakers and warm-up games are used to get the group comfortable with each other, the trainer and the subject. They can also be used to 'set the scene'.

The more physical games can be used to calm a group down when it first arrives in preparation for the work ahead. Similarly they can be used at anytime throughout the session to get rid of excess energy prior to focusing on more task-orientated exercises and activities and can be used to energise groups that are a little sleepy or sluggish, or between more concentrated 'thinking' sessions.

It is common to use one or two icebreakers at the start of a session and its useful to have a few 'standbys' in case the group loses interest or goes through them very quickly. As a general rule you should end whilst the group on a high. Make a point of building your repertoire so you always have something new up your sleeve. As you work with your group you will come to know which ones they enjoy and you will be able to judge quickly which game will work with which group. 'The New Youth Games Book' by Dearling and Armstrong (Russell House Publishing) is a very useful source of ideas.

Airlock

Purpose

✪ A quick and simple way to get the group calmed down and quiet at the start of the session.

✪ Reinforces the need for confidentiality in the group setting.

Who is it for?

✪ Good for new groups or large groups of young people with groups of 6-15 people.

Resources and staff required

✪ 1 staff member to facilitate, a volunteer from the group to time the silence.

Time allowed

✪ The airlock is a one-minute silence at the beginning and the end of the session.

Instructions

✪ Explain to your group that you are going to ask them to enter the session through an airlock.

✪ Explain they will also have to go back through the airlock when they leave the session later.

✪ Say that anything talked about or disclosed during the time between the entering and leaving is to be treated as confidential to the group and is not to be discussed outside the setting. Then ask them to enter the airlock.

✪ Ask a group member to keep the time and the group to be totally silent for one minute-no giggling either.

Handy hints

✪ This is much harder than it seems.

✪ Lots of groups manage about five seconds to start with.

✪ Make sure you repeat the exercise at the end of the session.

Good things – bad things

Purpose

- ✪ A simple exercise for the start of the session.
- ✪ To help the group feel more at ease.
- ✪ To find out about people's lives within the group.
- ✪ Helps group learn each other's names if they don't know each other, as well as giving the facilitator a chance to learn names.
- ✪ Gives everyone a chance to say something and to break the ice.

Who is it for?

- ✪ This icebreaker would work with groups of all ages (6-12 participants).

Resources and staff required

- ✪ 1 staff member.

Time allowed

- ✪ 5 minutes depending on the group size (Will take longer with larger groups).

Instructions

- ✪ Go round the group and get them to say one good thing and one bad thing that have happened to them during the last week. (These are not discussed at this stage).
- ✪ It simply gives the group members a chance to speak, think about other things in their lives and perhaps get something out in the open that has been bothering them.
- ✪ Offer space to discuss problems that come up at a later point perhaps at the end of the session, in privacy if needed.

Handy hints

- ✪ These can be as trivial or serious as the group wishes.
- ✪ Try to make it as quick as possible... it is an icebreaker.
- ✪ Generally the more you get to know your group, the more likely they are to reveal real problems or things that might be bothering them.
- ✪ If you want a more positive atmosphere or if the group are new to each other, you could miss out the bad thing.

Chair swap game (overdose)

Purpose

- To liven up group and to get participants going.
- To start the session with a bang.

Who is it for?

- For all age groups, with groups of 8 or more. This game seems to work well with quieter or less enthusiastic groups to get them warmed up and laughing at the beginning.
(Watch out for younger age groups as this can get extremely noisy and lively).

Resources and staff required

- 1 staff member.

Time allowed

- 5-10 minutes.

Instructions

- Get the group to sit on chairs in a circle with one person or yourself standing in the centre.
- There should be one chair less than the total number taking part, so that there is always one person to stand in the middle.
- The game simply requires the person in the centre to shout out a 'swap chairs if you...' command.
- The idea is for this person to grab a seat as the swaps happen, so leaving someone else in the centre. This will create mayhem as the members scrabble for seats.
- 'Swap chairs' commands can be left to the creativity of the groups but examples might include: swap seats if you...are wearing trainers...or...ate breakfast today...or...watched Coronation Street last night...or...got drunk last weekend...or are wearing black underwear...or...have a body piercing...or...like chocolate body paint etc. the list is endless!

Handy hints

- The dafter the better.
- Try and get everyone to join in.
- There is lots of variation you can use for this exercise.
- You can use lots of different topics.

Variations

- You can use 3 types of drinks e.g. Beer, Vodka, Alcopop.
- Go round the group and give each participant a name of a drink, Beer, Vodka, Alcopop, Beer, Vodka and so on...
- And if Cocktail is used everyone has to move and change seats.
- Same as before, but you only change seats if your drink is called.

Hammered
Young people and alcohol

Name game

Purpose

- ✪ Icebreaker, a good warm up game.
- ✪ To help the group feel more at ease.
- ✪ To find out about alcohol knowledge of group.
- ✪ Helps group learn each other's names if they don't know each other.
- ✪ Gives everyone a chance to say something and to break the ice.
- ✪ Gives the facilitator a chance to learn names.

Who is it for?

- ✪ All groups.

Resources and staff required

- ✪ 1 Facilitator.
- ✪ Name Game Alphabet sheet to help, if there are lots of names beginning with the same letter.

Time allowed

- ✪ 5 minutes (depending on group size).

Instructions

- ✪ The group is in a circle or facing the facilitator.
- ✪ The facilitators explains to the group that they have to think of a drink (This can be alcoholic or non-alcoholic drink) or something associated with alcohol which starts with the same letter as the first letter of their name and put it in front of it.
- ✪ The facilitator starts with their own name to give an example, Lager Laura, Alcopop Amanda etc.
- ✪ Go round the group with each participant having a shot. It helps people to remember names in the short term and usually create a few laughs. You also might discover a few new types of alcohol.

Handy hints

- ✪ Help individual if others in the group can't help.
- ✪ Try and make it as quick as possible... it is an icebreaker.
- ✪ If an individual is having trouble, ask others for help before offering suggestions.

Word association circle

Purpose

✪ A sequence game that works very well and is great to play.

Who is it for?

✪ Bigger groups, great with young people and adults.

Resources and staff required

✪ 1 staff member.

Time allowed

✪ 10 minutes.

Instructions

✪ Get the group to sit in a circle and practice a simple clapping rhythm e.g. clap clap space, clap clap space.

✪ Explain that a word has to be said aloud into the spaces as it goes around the circle.

✪ This word should be associated with the previous word spoken.

✪ The game can be played on different themes such as drugs or alcohol. An example start sequence could be:
Clap – clap larger. Clap – clap drunk. Clap – clap weekend. Clap – clap dancing. Clap – clap hangover. Clap – clap wine. Clap – clap party. Etc.

✪ Once the group have got the hang of this, forfeits can be added or people can be put out of the game if they fail to say an appropriate word in time.

Variations

✪ A variation is to work through the alphabet on particular themes e.g. cars, flowers, drinks. Clap – clap amaretto. Clap – clap beer. Clap – clap cola. Clap – clap Diamond White, etc.

This game was adapted from a popular drinking game where the forfeit was to drink 2 or 3 fingers of a chosen drink, thus getting very drunk in the process!

Stand up if...

Purpose

- ✪ To introduce the topic of alcohol to the group.
- ✪ To encourage active participation.

Who is it for?

- ✪ Good for tired or lazy groups, and can work with groups of 6-30 of any age.

Resources and staff required

- ✪ 1 staff member depending on the size of the group.

Time allowed

- ✪ 5 minutes.

Instructions

- ✪ Have the group sitting in a circle.
- ✪ Explain confidentiality and they don't have to take part if they don't want to.
- ✪ Say 'stand up if'... (See examples below).
- ✪ Allow 10 seconds for people to make their choice.
- ✪ Ask them to sit down again.

Examples: Stand up if...

    You skipped breakfast this morning

    You have ever had the tiniest sip of alcohol

    You have ever been drunk

    You have been drunk in the last 4 weeks

    You have ever been sick through alcohol

    You know what a unit of alcohol is

    Your favourite tipple is wine/beer

    You have ever got yourself into a risky situation through drink

Add statements as and when appropriate.

Handy hints

- ✪ Keep the pace fast.
- ✪ Make sure everyone joins in.
- ✪ Answers are not discussed.

Last week I...

Purpose

- ✪ To build trust in the group.
- ✪ To explore alcohol use within the group.

Who is it for?

- ✪ Groups of workers, peer educators, other youth groups (young people 16+).

Resources and staff required

- ✪ 1 Staff Member.

Time allowed

- ✪ 15 minutes.

Instructions

- ✪ Explain to the group that the next activity involves sharing with everyone else something about their own use of alcohol.
- ✪ Gather everyone into a large group, taking turns. It will help if the trainer/facilitator begins. An example might be:

  Pints of beer on Friday

  No reason, socialising with friends

  Loosened me up

- ✪ When this is finished, you could summarise the different reasons people had for using alcohol and the benefits and drawbacks they experienced. This could form the basis of a group discussion.

Handy hints

- ✪ Better to use this exercise when the group members know each other reasonably well.
- ✪ This exercise may be used to open up discussion on a number of issues, such as:

  The addictive potential of alcohol

  The reasons why people drink alcohol

  Getting the desired effect without using alcohol.

Hammered
Young people and alcohol

Alcohol bingo

Purpose

✪ A simple icebreaking exercise. It is an ideal exercise to get people talking to each other as well as introducing the topic of alcohol to the group.

Who is it for?

✪ For all age-groups.
✪ Works best with a group of 12 people or more.
✪ This exercise works well as an icebreaker with groups that do or do not know each other that well.

Resources and staff required

✪ 1 staff member depending on the size of the group.
✪ 1 Alcohol Bingo card for each group member.

Time allowed

✪ 10 minutes.

Instructions

✪ Participants walk around the room with their Alcohol Bingo card and the task is finding someone who agrees with the statement on the card.
✪ The winner is the first person to find someone different who can agree with the statement on the Alcohol Bingo sheet, so with effect if there are 12 participants, you should have 12 different names agreeing to the statements on your sheet.

Handy hints

✪ You can gear the statements to peoples' level of experience of alcohol, from minimal use of alcohol with younger teenagers to regular use of alcohol with older participants.

→

Find someone who has had a sip of alcohol	Find someone who has been sick through drinking alcohol	Find someone who has regretted something they did after drinking alcohol
Find someone who has had an alcoholic drink with their parents	Find someone who knows what a unit of alcohol is?	Find someone who started drinking before the age of 14
Find someone who knows how many units there are in a pint of ordinary strength beer?	Find someone who can name 3 types of alcohol	Find someone who doesn't like the taste of alcohol
Find someone who can name 2 other names for alcohol or getting drunk	Find someone who knows safe weekly drinking limits for young people	Find someone who has an older brother or sister that drinks alcohol
Find someone who knows how old you have to be to purchase alcohol?	Find someone who has a parent that drinks alcohol	Find someone who knows a cure for a hangover

Passing on information

The main purpose of the following exercises is to pass on information about alcohol and its effects in a fun, interactive and unbiased way.

They look at the hard facts about alcohol but can also be used to promote and extend discussions around the subject and also help you get your group working together.

Hammered
Young people and alcohol

Effects cards

Purpose

- This is a simple exercise to explore the effects that drinking alcohol can have on our bodies, the effects on what we do and the effects alcohol can have on other people.

Who is it for?

- This exercise can be used with a small group of 6-8 young people, upper primary school age (10-11 yrs).

Resources and staff required

- 1 staff member.
- Effects cards.

Time allowed

- 15 minutes.

Instructions

- Use the cards to present the statements to the group.
- The group should decide if the statement is a true or false effect of alcohol.
- Key points to make:
- Alcohol is a depressant drug that slows down reaction times and reduces inhibitions.
- Alcohol affects people differently.
- Too much alcohol at once can have very serious immediate effects.
- Too much alcohol over a period of time can have very serious effects on your health.

→

You become giggly

You feel dizzy and fall over

You end up kissing someone

You end up using lots of drugs

You turn blue

You feel really upset and start crying

You are sick

You can die

You start arguing with your friends or get into a fight

You get cancer

You can drown

You ruin your liver

Your hair falls out

You have a heart attack

You won't be able to stop drinking (become addicted)

You get arrested and put in jail

You can become giggly

True, lowered inhibitions, lack of self-control.

You end up kissing someone

True, this can happen-lowered inhibitions, lack of self-control.

You can turn blue

False, not unless you have drunk so much that you lose consciousness and stop breathing.

You are sick

True. Different people are sick on varying amounts of alcohol.

You start arguing with friends or get into a fight

True. It can happen because of lowered inhibitions and lack of self-control.

You can drown

False, you won't drown in alcohol. If you drink too much you might not be in control of what you are doing and if you fell in water you might not be able to swim well enough to save your life.

Your hair falls out

False, although if you drink excessively for a number of years it could cause your hair to thin.

You won't be able to stop drinking (become addicted)

False, not straight away. But drink regularly enough and often enough and your body will 'need' alcohol to function properly and you will be addicted.

You feel dizzy and can fall over

True

You end up using lots of drugs

False, not unless you choose to. Some people feel that after a while the 'buzz' they get from alcohol is not enough and turn to other drugs to get it.

You feel really upset and start crying

True- lowered inhibitions, lack of self-control. Drinking alcohol when you feel upset can make you feel even worse.

You can die

True. If you drink too much you can get alcoholic poisoning or go into a coma and possibly die. This is rare but does happen. You can also die from accidents while drunk.

You get cancer

True, excessive long term use will lead to cancers.

You ruin your liver

True, the liver cannot cope with long term excessive use and will be damaged.

You have a heart attack

False, but long term excessive use can increase your chances of having a heart attack.

You get arrested and put in jail

False, but drinking can affect your behaviour and you might do something that will lead to a situation where the police are involved.

Alcohol big body game

Purpose

- Quickly stimulates discussion about reasons for drinking.
- To look at general knowledge about alcohol and specifically its effect on the physiology of the body.
- Encourages group interaction.
- Involves everyone in the group and requires the group to move around.
- Creates a lively atmosphere where people feel able to talk freely.
- Allows swift evaluation of the knowledge levels of the group.

Who is it for?

- 12 to 16 year olds. (Can be done with adults too).
- Single gender or mixed groups.
- Best with groups of 4 to 8 but can work with 10 to 12 (working in pairs).

Resources and staff required

- 1 staff member to facilitate.
- Large sheets of card or paper (person sized).
- Question cards.
- Coloured marker pens.
- Back up notes for you to help with the awkward questions.

Time allowed

- Approximately 20-30 minutes, depending on size and availability of the group.

Instructions

- Divide participants into manageable groups and give each group a large sheet of card/ paper, markers and a set of question cards.
- Ask each group to choose a 'body' who has to lie down on the sheet of card.
- Get someone to draw their outline.
- The group should then work their way through the questions on the cards. Following the instructions and adding comments to the sheet of paper.

Handy hints

- The idea is to get people talking together, discussing the questions and the issues that arise. By the end of the session, the sheet should be covered in words and drawings.
- Once the group has done as much as they can, go through all the questions with them correcting, explaining and checking out that everyone understands the responses.
- The game requires factual knowledge on the part of the worker. Be sure you know the answers yourself first (see the section on Alcohol Information).

Variations

- The game can be varied by being played individually using a smaller body drawn on a sheet of paper.

→

Instruction/question cards

1. How is the body affected by alcohol? What is the difference between the effect on male and female bodies?

Task
Write or draw the effects on the body.

5. Which parts of the body are damaged by too much alcohol? Note any differences between men and women.

Task
Write on the body, labelling the parts where they are found.

2. What is the name we use for the measurement of alcohol consumption?

Task
Write the answer beside the body.

6. Why do you think young people drink?

Task
Write all the reasons you can think of around the body. Note any difference between men and women.

3. How long does it take the body to break down one unit of alcohol?

Task
Write the answer beside the body.

7. Where is alcohol broken down in the body?

Task
Mark on the body where this happens and label the parts.

4. How many units of alcohol are there in the following drinks? A pint of cider, a glass of wine, a vodka and coke, a bottle of diamond white cider, a double whisky. Take a guess if you don't know.

Task
Write the answer beside the body.

8. How much is too much? What is the maximum that women and men should drink as recommended by the Government?

Task
Write the answer beside the body.

One for the road

Purpose

- ✪ The exercise is designed to make the young people aware of the effects of alcohol.
- ✪ It looks at young people's experiences and knowledge of the effects of alcohol.

Who is it for?

- ✪ Young people aged 11-16 years old.
- ✪ For groups of 8-12 people.

Resources and staff required

- ✪ 1-2 staff members.
- ✪ Plastic cups, soft drinks, flipchart paper and marker pens.

Time allowed

- ✪ 20-30 minutes.

Instructions

- ✪ Pour the soft drink into a couple of plastic cups.
- ✪ Then ask the young people to come up and take a sip of the drink – pretending its alcohol – then act out an effect that alcohol can have.
- ✪ Do not lead the young people at this moment; let them draw on their own knowledge and experiences.
- ✪ As each effect is acted out, write it down on flipchart paper. Young people will usually come up with the negative effects of alcohol.
- ✪ Once everyone has participated, go through the effects that have been written on the paper and draw a smiley face against all the good effects and a sad face against all the bad effects – get the young people to call them out. In general the majority will be bad effects. If that is the case, ask them why they might drink alcohol if they recorded more bad effects than good effects. Ask if non-alcoholic drinks are acceptable as an alternative.

→

One for the road - contd.

Suggestions for advantages and disadvantages of alcohol when discussing with young people:

Advantages	Disadvantages
• Relaxation and confidence • A wide range of drinks to suit all tastes • Social activity with friends and family	• Higher risk of casual sex leading to pregnancies and spread of Sexually Transmitted Infections • Socially inappropriate actions, bad jokes, dreadful chat up lines, arguments, fights, vomiting, petty crime, going further than you want with your girl/ boyfriend. • Risk of accidents at work, home or on the road • Criminal activity linked to drinking

Cunning cocktails

Purpose
- ✪ Stimulates discussion.
- ✪ A great way to pass on information without 'lecturing'.
- ✪ A fun exercise.

Who is it for?
- ✪ Anyone over 16 years.

Resources and staff required
- ✪ Question sheets.
- ✪ Pens.
- ✪ A prize for the winner.
- ✪ 1 staff member (facilitator).

Time allowed
- ✪ 20 minutes-1¹/₂ hrs.

Instructions
- ✪ Give out questionnaires and pens.
- ✪ Remind them it is not a test and that they don't need to put their names on it.
- ✪ Allow 5-10 minutes to complete.
- ✪ Go through the answers elaborating with facts figures, anecdotes and harm reduction advice. Give 1 point for each correct answer.
- ✪ Present the prize to the winner.

Keep this exercise as interactive as possible. Ask participants what they think the answers are and why.

Handy hints
- ✪ This exercise often generates many questions, read up on your alcohol information and make sure that you are comfortable with it.
- ✪ Don't forget to keep an eye on the time.
- ✪ Regularly check and update the questions and answers.

Variations
- ✪ This exercise can be done using various methods such as the answers can be presented as an OHP or PowerPoint presentation, if this is appropriate to your group.
- ✪ Add and subtract questions to make the quiz relevant for the type of group you are working with.

→

Hammered
Young people and alcohol

What do you really know about alcohol?

Tick the correct answer for each question. There is only ONE correct answer.

1. **About how much does the government get from taxes on alcohol each year?**
   a) £11.5 billion
   b) £270 million
   c) Nothing – it is all given to charity

2. **Most violent crime is committed by people under the influence of alcohol.**
   TRUE or FALSE

3. **An average glass of wine has as much alcohol in it as:**
   a) $\frac{1}{2}$ glass sherry
   b) 1 pint lager
   c) $\frac{1}{4}$ can of Carlsberg special
   d) 4 liqueur chocolates

4. **Women get drunk more quickly than men on the same amount of alcohol because:**
   a) They are better at drinking
   b) They wear high heels
   c) They have less fluid and more fat in their bodies

5. **Young females consume less alcohol than young males.**
   TRUE OR FALSE

6. **How many calories are in an average pint of beer?**
   a) 180
   b) none
   c) 300

7. **Alcohol is a stimulant and livens people up.**
   TRUE or FALSE

8. **Putting lemonade in your malt whisky:**
   a) Causes the drink to have less effect
   b) Is a complete waste of good whisky
   c) Has no effect on the alcohol content

→

9. **In the league table of how much alcohol is consumed in different countries worldwide, the UK comes:**
   a) top
   b) 5th
   c) 21st

10. **Alcohol kills more people each year than illegal drugs do.**
    TRUE or FALSE

11. **Long term damage from heavy use of alcohol affects men earlier.**
    TRUE or FALSE

12. **It is illegal to give a young person under 14 a drink.**
    TRUE or FALSE

13. **A hangover is caused by mixing your drinks.**
    TRUE or FALSE

14. **A colleague goes to the pub, they have 6 pints of beer and then leave at midnight to go home. How long is the alcohol in their system?**
    a) 6 hours
    b) 12 hours
    c) 16 hours

15. **If they then had to drive to work at 7am the following day they would be within the legal limit?**
    TRUE OR FALSE

→

The answers

Thanks for filling in the questionnaire. These are the answers. Check out how well you did.

1. **About how much does the government get from taxes on alcohol each year?**
    £11.5 billion. This is an approximate figure based on statistics from 2000.

2. **Most violent crime is committed by people under the influence of alcohol.**
    TRUE. Research has shown that drinking plays a part in 30% of sexual offences, 44% of domestic violence, 50% of street crime and 85% of crime in pubs and clubs.

3. **An average glass of wine has as much alcohol in it as a quarter of a can of Carlsberg Special.**
    Surprised? Many people don't know how much alcohol is in different drinks. A rough guide is; half a pint of normal beer or lager = 1 glass of wine = 1 whisky = 1 glass of sherry (all standard "pub" measures).

4. **Women get drunk more quickly than men on the same amount of alcohol because they have less fluid and more fat in their bodies.**
    This means that alcohol gets more concentrated in their bodies, and they feel the effects for longer. This doesn't mean that men don't have to watch what they drink!

5. **Young females consume less alcohol than young males.**
    FALSE. Recent studies show that they consume more. This will be highlighted using the statistics of recent research during the course of today.

6. **How many calories are in an average pint of beer?**
    180. Remember alcohol contains a lot of calories for very little nutritional value.

7. **Alcohol is a stimulant and livens people up.**
    FALSE. Initially, you may feel livelier after a drink, because it can stop you feeling embarrassed. But the alcohol actually has a depressant effect on your nervous system i.e. it slows it down. (lots of people mistake its early effect for a stimulant).

8. **Putting lemonade in your malt whisky has no effect on the alcohol content.**
    It might be a waste of good whisky, but it certainly doesn't affect the amount of alcohol in the drink. Remember also that fizzy mixers can actually speed up the alcohol effect causing alcohol to be absorbed more quickly.

→

9. **In the league table of how much alcohol is consumed in different countries, the UK comes 21st.**

   In 1991 France consumed the equivalent of 12.4 litres of pure alcohol per person, while the UK only knocked back 7.3 litres! However our consumption has gone up over the last 10 years while France's has gone down.

10. **Alcohol kills more people each year than illegal drugs do.**

    TRUE. Despite what you may hear, alcohol is a far greater killer than illegal drugs. In 2001, 1103 people died from alcohol misuse (although this figure does not include traffic accidents). Drugs accounted for 384 deaths in 2002.

11. **Long term damage from heavy use of alcohol affects men earlier.**

    FALSE. Affects show more rapidly in women than men especially with brain damage, stomach cancer.

12. **It is illegal to give a young person under 14 a drink.**

    FALSE. It is not illegal to give someone under 14 a drink. However, it is illegal to do so in a bar. Young people under 14 are not allowed in a bar unless it has a refreshment license and they are accompanied by an adult. You can't give a child under 5 a drink unless under medical supervision or in an emergency. It is also illegal to buy a drink for someone under 18. For over 16s they can go into a bar and buy a drink with a meal (beer, wine, cider, sherry, port) in the part of the premises where food is served.

13. **A hangover is caused by mixing your drinks.**

    FALSE. Hangovers are only caused by poisoning, dehydration and low blood sugars.

14. **A colleague goes to the pub they have 6 pints of beer and then leave at midnight to go home. How long is the alcohol in their system?**

    12 hours. It takes the body approximately 1 hour to get rid of the alcohol contained in a half pint of beer. Therefore it will take the body approximately 12 hours to get rid of the alcohol contained in 6 pints of beer.

15. **If they then had to drive to work at 7am the following day they would be within the legal limit.**

    FALSE. The body would still have the equivalent of 5 units of alcohol. (During the night the metabolism slows down).

Dry bar?

Purpose

- To provide an alcohol free party.
- Includes everyone in the group.
- To encourage creativity.
- It provides a fun and credible focus for chat and socialising.

Who is it for?

- An activity to be run with young people 11-16 years old. Ideal with groups of up to 12 people.

Resources and staff required

- A wide range of fruit juices from the cocktail menu.
- Cocktail cherries.
- Parasols.
- Slices of lemon and lime.
- Bottles of soft drinks, from the cocktail menu.
- 2 staff to help facilitate.

Time allowed

- 30-45 minutes.

Instructions

- It should be set up by a group of the young people and is run by them.
- The group make up the cocktails from the recipes, or create their own.

Handy hints

- This dry bar concept has proven to be a great success and it can be drunk dry on occasions!
- Make sure you have enough soft drinks available.

Variations

- Encourage the young people to invent their own concoctions. It is a great way for others to get involved and relationships to be built.

→

COCKTAIL LIST

Measures
One single measure is 25ml = 2.5cl
measures of 1/6 gill (23.6ml)
I teaspoon = 1/6th measure
1 dash = 1/10th teaspoon

1. Bingo

Ingredients

1 msr papaya juice

1 msr orange juice

1 msr coconut cream

1 msr pineapple juice

$^1/_2$ msr lime juice

1 msr strawberry puree

$^1/_4$ msr grenadine

Method

Blend briefly with a glassful of crushed ice, add straws.

2. Bitter Experience

Ingredients

2 msr orange juice

$^1/_2$ msr lime juice

2 msr sparkling bitter lemon

Method

Add to glass filled with broken ice, add short straws.

3. Fruit Fairy

Ingredients

2 msr pineapple juice

1 msr coconut cream

$^1/_2$ msr banana syrup

3 tablespoons vanilla ice-cream

Method

Blend briefly. Garnish with a slice of banana and a cherry.

→

Hammered
Young people and alcohol

4. Strawberry Kiss

Ingredients

3 msr strawberry puree
1¹/₂ msr pineapple juice
¹/₂ msr lemon juice
¹/₂ msr whipping cream
¹/₂ teaspoon caster sugar

Method

Blend briefly with half a glassful of crushed ice.
Garnish with half a caster sugar coated strawberry.

5. Tarzan's Juicy Cooler

Ingredients

3 msr orange juice
3 msr pineapple juice
¹/₄ msr grenadine
¹/₂ msr lemon juice
1 tablespoon strawberry yoghurt
2 teaspoons clear honey

Method

Blend briefly with half a glassful of crushed ice.
Garnish with a slice of orange speared with a cherry.

6. Mickey Mouse

Ingredients

1¹/₂ msr cold cola
1 tablespoon vanilla ice-cream
1 msr whipped cream

Method

Add cola, then ice-cream to ice filled glass.
Top with the whipped cream.
Garnish with two cherries and grated chocolate.
Serve on a napkin with straws.

7. Tiger Tim

Ingredients

Grapefruit juice
Lemon juice
Lemonade

Method

Half fill a glass with grapefruit juice.
Add a dash of lemon and top up with lemonade.
Finish with a slice of lemon and a straw.

8. Strawberry Fields

Ingredients

Strawberry syrup
Lemon juice
Apple juice
Ginger ale

Method

Pour a measure of strawberry syrup and a dash of
lemon juice into a glass.
Half fill with apple juice.
Top up with ginger ale.

9. Sunset

Ingredients

Orange juice

Lemonade

Grenadine

Method

Half fill the glass with orange juice.

Top up with lemonade.

Pour one measure of Grenadine gently into the glass.

Finish with a slice of orange slit partially down the middle and hung on the side of the glass, a parasol and a straw.

10. Foursquare

Ingredients

Apple juice

Lemon juice

Orange juice

Pineapple juice

Method

Quarter fill a glass with apple juice.

Add quarter of a glass of orange juice.

Add quarter of a glass of pineapple juice.

Add quarter of a glass of lemon juice.

Finish with slices of apple, orange, lemon and pineapple.

11. Banana Boat

Ingredients

$1/2$ mashed banana

3 msr milk

1 msr pineapple juice

1 msr coconut cream

Method

Blend briefly with half a glassful of crushed ice.

Garnish with slice of banana and a cherry.

12. Tropicana

Ingredients

1msr blue Curacao

1msr coconut

Dash of lemon

Pineapple juice

Soda water

Method

Into a glass pour 1msr blue Curacao, 1msr. of coconut and a dash of lemon.

Top up glass with pineapple juice and soda water.

Serve with a cherry on a red parasol and straw.

Cross, Robert (1996) *The Classic 1000 Cocktails*. Foulsham. London.

Hammered
Young people and alcohol

The quiz aboot bevvy (11-14 year olds)

Purpose

- ✪ Stimulates discussion.
- ✪ A great way to pass on information in a fun manner.

Who is it for?

- ✪ Young people (11-14 year olds).
- ✪ Groups of 8-15 members.

Resources and staff required

- ✪ Question sheets.
- ✪ Pens.
- ✪ A prize for the winner.
- ✪ 1 facilitator.

Time allowed

- ✪ 30 minutes.

Instructions

- ✪ Give out quiz sheet and pens.
- ✪ Allow 10-15 minutes to complete.
- ✪ Go through the answers elaborating with facts and harm reduction advice. Give points to each correct answer.
- ✪ Present the prize to the winner.

Handy hints

- ✪ Keep this exercise as interactive as possible.
- ✪ Ask the participants what they think the answers are and why.
- ✪ This exercise often generates further questions so facilitator needs to read up on alcohol information.

→

1. Name three white spirits.

2. Name three foreign lagers.

3. Name a country that vodka comes from.

4. How many nips in a standard bottle of vodka?

5. If you put cola in your vodka what happens?
    a) It increases the alcohol level
    b) You get drunk quicker
    c) Stops you getting a hangover

6. How many pints of lager can you drink and still drive safely?
    a) 2 pints
    b) 3$\frac{1}{2}$ pints
    c) none

7. Which organ of the body breaks down alcohol?
    a) Appendix
    b) Liver
    c) Brain

8. It's legal to drink alcohol at what age?
    a) 5
    b) 14
    c) 18

9. What could happen if the police find you drinking on the street?
    a) They might invite you to a party
    b) They could arrest you and take you to jail
    c) Confiscate your alcohol and inform your parents

10. What should you do if your friend collapses after drinking alcohol?
    a) Put them in the recovery position
    b) If at all possible don't leave them alone
    c) Make sure that they are safe
    d) All of the above

→

The answers

1. Name three white spirits
   Rum, Vodka, Gin, Tequila

2. Name three foreign lagers
   XXXX, Fosters, Stella Artois, Carlsberg, Grolsch, Kronenbourg, Miller, Budweiser, Becks, Heineken

3. Name a country that vodka comes from
   Russia, Sweden, Finland, Denmark, Norway

4. How many nips in a standard bottle of vodka?
   36

5. If you put cola in your vodka what happens?
   a) It increases the alcohol level
   b) You get drunk quicker
   c) Stops you getting a hangover

6. How many pints of lager can you drink and still drive safely?
   a) 2 pints
   b) 3¹/₂ pints
   c) none

7. Which organ of the body breaks down alcohol?
   a) Appendix
   b) Liver
   c) Brain

8. It's legal to drink alcohol at what age?
   a) 5
   b) 14
   c) 18

9. What could happen if the police find you drinking on the street?
   a) They might invite you to a party
   b) They could arrest you and take you to jail
   c) Confiscate your alcohol and inform your parents

10. What should you do if your friend collapses after drinking alcohol?
    a) Put them in the recovery position
    b) If at all possible don't leave them alone
    c) Make sure that they are safe
    d) All of the above

The knowledge (16 plus year olds)

Purpose

- ✪ Stimulates discussion about units and cost implications for young people.
- ✪ A fun way of passing on information.

Who is it for?

- ✪ Young people aged 16 and above.
- ✪ Groups of 8-12 people.

Resources and staff required

- ✪ Quiz sheets.
- ✪ Pens.
- ✪ Flip Chart.
- ✪ A prize for the winner.
- ✪ 1 Facilitator.

Time allowed

- ✪ 30-45 minutes (depending on the amount of discussion).

Instructions

- ✪ Have a 'drinks box' with examples of the drinks in the quiz available for young people to check the labels.
- ✪ Hand out the quiz sheets and pens.
- ✪ Allow 15 minutes to complete.
- ✪ Go through the answers, explaining how the units were calculated and identify the costs of specific drinks according to the young people's knowledge.
- ✪ Elaborate on facts and harm reduction messages i.e. mixing drinks, mixing downers, keeping safe- keeping an eye on drinks; drink spiking, drink water and soft drinks in-between alcoholic drinks etc.
- ✪ Stimulate discussion – were the young people surprised by the amount of units in certain drinks? What about the cost of alcohol? Are some drinks quite cheap? Do you think alcohol should be illegal?

Handy hints

- ✪ Use empty or dummy bottles in your 'drinks box' if you have concerns that your young people might 'help themselves' or want a taster.
- ✪ Check prices at local off-licences so you know roughly the current prices of drinks.

→

Hammered
Young people and alcohol

✪ Before handing out the quiz sheets to the group of young people, it is useful to deliver a short presentation on Flip chart paper exploring What is a unit? – How a unit is calculated? The ethanol unit calculation formula:

$$1 \text{ unit} = \frac{\text{Volume of drink (ml) x \% ABV (percentage alcohol)}}{1000}$$

What does this look like?

1 unit = 1 measure of spirits (25ml) = 1 small glass of wine (8% 125ml) = ½ pint of ordinary strength lager (3.5%).

Many 500 ml cans of strong beer or cider (9%) contain 4 units of alcohol.
A bottle of 11% wine = 8 units
A bottle of 40% vodka = 28 units
A 3 litre bottle (9%) white cider = 27 units

Once the young people have a general understanding about units and the differences between men and women in the consumption of alcohol, safe drinking levels for women, men and young people and a look at the cost implications for young people, and then move onto the quiz.

Units of alcohol everyday

Limits for Adult Men	Limits for Adult Women
1-3 units (Safe for most adult men)	1-2 units (Safe for most adult women)
4-5 units (Risky)	3 units (Risky)
6-7 units (Dangerous)	4-5 units (Dangerous)
8-10 units (Harms health very badly)	6-10 units (Harms health very badly)

A quiz about units

How many units of alcohol are in the following drinks and how much would they cost?

1. A 700 ml bottle of Merrydown cider?

2. A 275ml bottle of WKD Blue?

3. A 750 ml bottle of Buckfast?

4. A ¼ bottle Smirnoff vodka and 2 cans of Red Bull?

5. 3 bottles of Smirnoff Ice?

6. A 2 ltr bottle of Strongbow cider and a 500ml bottle of After Shock?

7. 2 bottles of reef and 3 bottles of WKD Irn Bru?

8. A 700ml bottle of Lambrini, a packet of wine gums and a ¼ bottle of Smirnoff vodka?

→

Hammered
Young people and alcohol

A quiz about units: the answers

How many units of alcohol are in the following drinks?

	Alcohol %	Units	Cost
A 700ml bottle of Merrydown cider	7.5% ABV	5	
A 275ml bottle of WKD Blue	5.5% ABV	1.5	
A 750ml bottle of Buckfast	17% ABV	12.75	
A ¼ bottle Smirnoff vodka and 2 cans of Red Bull	35% ABV	9	
3 bottles of Smirnoff Ice	5.5% ABV	4.5	
A 2 ltr bottle of Strongbow cider and a 500ml bottle of After Shock	3.5% ABV 40% ABV	27	
2 bottles of Reef and 3 bottles of WKD Irn Bru	5.5% ABV	7.5	
A 700ml bottle of Lambrini, a packet of wine gums and a ¼ bottle of Smirnoff vodka	7.5% ABV 37% ABV	14	

Key information on alcohol, young people and the law

Purpose

✪ A useful exercise to explore issues around young people, alcohol and the law.

Who is it for?

✪ Young people (12-16 yrs).

Resources and staff required

✪ 1 member of staff.
✪ Alcohol, young people and the law paragraph.
✪ Pens.
✪ A prize for the winner.

Time allowed

✪ 15 minutes to complete paragraph.
✪ 10-20 minutes follow up discussion.

Instructions

✪ This exercise gives you a paragraph with missing key words. The missing key words are listed at the bottom of the page.
✪ Participants must decide which key words are placed into which blank space.
✪ The words at the bottom of this page can only be used once.

Handy hints

✪ This exercise can be used to ascertain the young people's base knowledge in this area.
✪ The exercise can be made more interactive by choosing members of the group to read out parts of the paragraph with their chosen answers.
✪ Facilitator may want to make up a discussion sheet with follow up questions. The exercise can then be followed by an in-depth discussion about the issues surrounding young people and the law, in relation to alcohol. The facilitator can highlight key points of the law.
✪ This exercise can be done individually or in small groups.

→

Hammered
Young people and alcohol

Only when young people are aged___ can they be _____ to be able to buy alcohol anywhere, as some ___have this as an age limit, although at 18 you can legally buy ___ in the majority of places, including off-licences.

Beer or cider, when accompanying a meal can be bought by anybody aged___, but not in a ___ If a YP is under ___ they cannot enter a bar unless the bar has a _____ _____. If it does not have one, they can go into parts of a _____ _____ where alcohol is either sold but not _____. e.g. an off-licence or a sales point away from the pub ___ drunk but not sold e.g. a garden or family room. _____ year olds can go into a pub but cannot drink alcohol, they must be accompanied by an ____. It is against the ___for anyone over 18 to buy alcohol for minors if they are under 18. This applies to licensed premises and off-sales.

If a _____ finds a YP in a public place with alcohol, and ____ that the person is under 18, then he can confiscate it. If they are over 18 and they suspect they may be supplying or buying it for under 18's they can again confiscate it.

If a YP is over ___ and are unable to look after themselves, then the police can take them into ___ for their own protection, they can then be ____ to the____ _____ for being drunk and incapable. If they are under 16 the police will take them to their home address, if that cannot be confirmed then they will take them to the nearest police station until a guardian can be contacted. The police may put a ____ to the ____ _____ or_____ _____ _____ regarding their drunkenness.

Use words only once in each space

Social work department	alcohol	constable	14
children's panel	report	14 and 15	guaranteed
children's certificate	reported	16	pub
licensed premises	custody	16 and 17	suspects
drunk	law	21	adult
bar	clubs	procurator fiscal	
		(Crown Prosecution Service)	

→

Key information on alcohol, young people and the law – contd.

Answers

Only when young people are aged **21** can they be **guaranteed** to be able to buy alcohol anywhere, as some **clubs** have this as an age limit, although at 18 you can legally buy **alcohol** in the majority of places, including off-licences.

Beer or cider when accompanying a meal can be bought by anybody aged **16 and 17**, but not in a **bar/pub**. If a YP is under **14** they cannot enter a bar unless the bar has a **children's certificate**. If it does not have one, they can go into parts of a **licensed premise** where alcohol is either sold but not **drunk**. e.g. an off-licence or a sales point away from the pub or drunk but not sold e.g. a garden or family room. **14 and 15** year olds can go into a pub but cannot drink alcohol; they must be accompanied by an **adult**. It is against the **law** for anyone over 18 to buy alcohol for minors if they are under 18. This applies to licensed premises and off-sales.

If a **constable** finds a YP in a public place with alcohol, and **suspects** that the person is under 18, then he can confiscate it. If they are over 18 and they suspect they may be supplying or buying it for under 18's they can again confiscate it.

If a YP is over **16** and are unable to look after themselves, then the police can take them into **custody** for their own protection, they can then be **reported** to the **procurator fiscal** for being drunk and incapable. If they are under 16 the police will take them to their home address, if that cannot be confirmed then they will take them to the nearest police station until a guardian can be contacted. The police may put a **report** to the **Children's Panel** or **Social Work department** regarding their drunkenness.

Challenging attitudes

These exercises explore what people think and feel about alcohol. They are designed to draw out people's opinions in a safe manner and to get them to think about their own attitudes to drinking.

The exercises offer a starting point for discussion, to examine and explore stereotypes. There are no right or wrong answers and discussion of this kind can often be very effective in enlightening and raising awareness.

Discussion will frequently challenge young people's beliefs and value base, so tactful facilitation is required.

Blitzed

Purpose

- ✪ Quickly stimulates discussion.
- ✪ Requires little factual knowledge, focus is on attitudes.
- ✪ Involves everyone and puts a value on each person's contribution.
- ✪ Permits quick evaluation of a group's views on drinking.

Who is it for?

- ✪ 12 years and over.
- ✪ Single gender or mixed groups.
- ✪ Groups of 6 to 12 people.

Resources and staff required

- ✪ Copies of the questionnaire.
- ✪ Pens.
- ✪ 1-2 staff; one person to read out statements and facilitate discussion and the other if need be to play devils advocate.

Time allowed

- ✪ 20 minutes.

Instructions

- ✪ Give everyone a copy of the questionnaire and a pen.
- ✪ Explain that the game is about what people think of drinking. There are no right or wrong answers.
- ✪ Each person should complete the questionnaire as quickly as possible putting one tick for each question. Gut reactions are best! Allow 5 minutes for completion of the questionnaire.

Each or selected questions can be discussed in more detail. Discussion will be more fruitful when there are strongly differing opinions within the group. The group facilitator might wish to highlight apparent inconsistencies of opinion within the group.

Handy hints

- ✪ Although the focus is on attitudes and not knowledge, questions may arise that require factual answers.
- ✪ The group facilitators attitudes may come into question by the participants.
- ✪ It is useful to have at least one "example" for each of the statements that can be quoted if necessary.

→

Hammered
Young people and alcohol

Variations

- The exercise can either be played in small groups with comments taken back to the big group, or as a whole group exercise.
- Statements from the questionnaire could be used and discussed individually. Each person in the group is given one statement (cut them up into strips and place in a hat, ask each person to pull one out). Each person reads out his or her statement and says what they think about it. The rest of the group can then offer their views. This works well in smaller groups and doesn't give the opportunity to use the don't know option. Everybody usually has something to say. It does, however, put individuals in the spotlight.

→

Attitudes towards drinking

Tick ONE box for each statement.

There are no right or wrong answers. It's your opinion that counts.

		Agree	Don't know	Disagree
1.	Being able to hold your drink is a sign of maturity.			
2.	Parties aren't the same without a good drink.			
3.	Alcoholics are a waste of everyone's time and money.			
4.	Boys find it harder to say "no" due to pressure to drink from their friends.			
5.	A woman who is drunk is a disgusting sight.			
6.	Alcohol companies shouldn't be involved in sports sponsorship.			
7.	It's out of order to shave someone's eyebrows when they are drunk.			
8.	Most people's lives revolve around drink.			
9.	Girls who get drunk are more likely to get taken advantage of sexually by boys.			
10.	It's better to take legal drugs like alcohol than illegal ones like Ecstasy.			
11.	There's no point in going into a pub if you are only going to drink orange juice all night.			
12.	Most people drink before they are 18 so you may as well reduce the age limit for drinking in pubs.			

Hammered
Young people and alcohol

'Alcohol is double trouble'

This exercise is very similar to 'Blitzed' but is more energetic and works well with the younger groups.

Purpose

- ✪ Encouraging people to discuss issues knowing that their views are listened to.
- ✪ To allow young people to have and express their own views.
- ✪ To begin to explore different attitudes.
- ✪ To have fun.

Who is it for?

- ✪ This can be used with different age groups but works really well with under 13 year olds.

Resources and staff required

- ✪ 1 facilitator per group.
- ✪ 3 cards with one of the following written on each: Agree, Disagree, Don't Know.
- ✪ Make space as there is a lot of movement.

Time allowed

- ✪ This can vary from 10 – 30 minutes (for a better discussion).

Instructions

- ✪ Have one person standing at each end of the room holding a card, 'agree' or 'disagree'.
- ✪ Explain to the young people that you are going to read out a statement and if they agree they should stand beside the agree person and likewise with disagree. If they don't know they should stand in the middle next to the don't know card.
- ✪ Get young people to stand in the middle of the room.
- ✪ Read out one of the statements from the 'Blitzed' sheet.
- ✪ Explain that there are no right or wrong answers and that they should not spend too much time thinking about it.
- ✪ When they have made their choice ask them to explain why.
- ✪ Get them to try and persuade the other group to come over to their side.

Handy hints

- ✪ Try to go beyond discussing the statement and get into some of the surrounding issues.
- ✪ Be aware that it can get noisy, so keep control of the group!

Down the local

Purpose

- This is a light-hearted way of looking at the realities of young people's drinking patterns.
- It is a good way of encouraging participation, since everyone can take part in making the maps.
- It offers a good way of opening up discussion and exploring issues in a non-threatening way.

Who is it for

- Any age.
- Mixed or single sex groups.
- Best in groups of 8-12, but possible with larger groups.

Resources and staff required

- Felt pens.
- Old magazines and glue.
- Scissors.
- Large sheets of paper.
- 2 staff to assist young people.

Time allowed

- 30 minutes.

Instructions

- Divide the group into smaller groups of 4 or 5 and give out magazines, pens, paper and scissors.
- Ask each group to create a map of their town/village/community showing the main landmarks, including their own homes.
- They should then mark on the places where people 'drink'. These should include recognised settings such as pubs, hotels and clubs, but also any other informal places such as parks, cemeteries, streets where young people are more likely to drink. As much humour, imagination and caricature as possible should be used in building up the maps.

Once the maps are complete, they can be compared and people asked to comment. Discussion could centre around:

- Do young people and adults drink in the same places? If not why not?
- Are some places better (safer, more enjoyable) than others?
- What are the pros and cons of drinking in the open air?

Handy hints

- It is possible that young people may be reluctant to reveal their drinking haunts. If this occurs the game will still work well by depicting the more recognised venues.

Hammered
Young people and alcohol

What's the message? Bottles and advert

Purpose

- To understand some ways in which the media can influence attitudes to drinking alcohol.
- To look at the purpose of advertising.
- Encourage young people to discuss alcoholic drinks advertising.

Who is it for?

- Young people (14 years +).
- 6-10 young people.

Resources and staff required

- 1-2 Facilitators.
- A 'drinks box' containing a variety of bottles and cans.
- Drinks adverts (cut from magazines or video clips).
- Magazines and Newspapers.
- TV and video.
- Glue.
- Flipchart paper.
- Pens.

Time allowed

- 30-40 minutes.

Instructions

- Divide into small groups and give each group a bottle and an advert.
- Discuss the following issues within each group and feedback to the main group.

Handy hints

Explore the power of advertising. Think about:

- What messages are the drink advertisements attempting to convey?
- What does the advert/label say about the drink and the person drinking it?
- Who is the drink/advert aimed at? Is it aimed at young people?
- Who drinks this?
- Does it appeal to you/others your age?
- What might happen to your behaviour if you drank this?

Draw out what advertisements do not do, for example;

- That you get drunk.
- That too much alcohol can damage your health.
- Don't provide the full picture, i.e. look at health consequences and the social consequences.

→

Hammered
Young people and alcohol

Variations

- As a follow on, the young people could go on to do the exercise Down the Local that looks at the places where adults and young people drink.
- Design an advertisement for a new alcoholic drink. The advert must tell the truth about what the drink will do to someone who drinks it (good and bad), tell the truth about the risks of drinking, and suggest what sort of people might drink this product. The finished product may be a magazine article, a TV advert, a radio advert or designing a leaflet.

The great piss up

Purpose

- ✪ Stimulates discussion.
- ✪ Lets the young people talk about issues at their level.
- ✪ Explores the bigger picture from health issues to governmental policy.
- ✪ A fun exercise.

Who is it for?

- ✪ Young people 13 and over.

Resources and staff required

- ✪ Space for a debate.
- ✪ Factsheets on alcohol, for example health issues, alcohol industry etc. (Alcohol Concern have a good range online: www.alcoholconcern.org.uk).
- ✪ 1 staff/volunteer to help organise and observe.

Time allowed

- ✪ 20 minutes-1¹/₂ hours.

Instructions

- ✪ Divide your group in half and explain you are going to have an important debate that will inform new Government policy.
- ✪ One side is to put forward the motion that 'alcohol should be made illegal'. If they are successful it will be an offence to sell, possess and consume alcohol. Effectively it will become a class A drug.
- ✪ The other group is to oppose this.
- ✪ Both groups should spend time (10mins to ¹/₂ hour depending on how much time you have overall) preparing their argument. They can use fact sheets for a more in-depth argument and if you have time.
- ✪ Begin the debate by letting the first side put forward their proposal. Allot a set amount of time.
- ✪ Let the other group counter the proposal for an equivalent length of time.
- ✪ The debate can proceed between the groups, making sure each group has the same time allowance.
- ✪ At the end of the exercise take a vote on the motion.
- ✪ A majority will pass the motion; a hung or minority vote for the motion will maintain the status quo.
- ✪ Try to keep some time aside to deconstruct the debate and widen out the issues.

→

The great piss up - contd.

Handy hints

✪ Keep an eye on the time and be aware that the debate might become heated.

✪ Young people sometimes find it difficult to wait their turn to speak. Be prepared to let the debate run and correct misinformation at the end.

✪ For variations, try having a panel in the form of a 'Question Time' debate. Two for banning alcohol and two against. Have the 'audience' ask pertinent questions. Your group of young people will have to be fairly confident in themselves and with each other for this to work well.

Tackling situations

These exercises are used to tackle potential situations young people may find themselves in.

They will stimulate discussion and demonstrate the choices young people have in drinking situations.

The exercises will boost confidence through allowing the young people to 'practise' handling situations and making the right choices to prevent harm.

Drinking scenarios

Purpose

- ❂ Stimulates discussion and encourages group interaction.
- ❂ Involves everyone in the group and requires the group to move around.

Who is it for?

- ❂ 12 to 16 year olds.
- ❂ Single gender or mixed groups.
- ❂ Best with groups of 6 to 12. Split larger groups into more manageable sizes.

Resources and staff required

- ❂ Drinking scenario cards.
- ❂ 1-2 staff/volunteers to facilitate and mingle between groups.

Time allowed

- ❂ 30 minutes, more time may be needed if the group want to act out the scenarios, depending on size, abilities and interest levels of your group.

Instructions

- ❂ Hand out the cards to the group(s) and ask people to read out the situations.
- ❂ Use these as the basis for group discussion.
- ❂ Aim to reach a consensus within the group on the actions, behaviours and outcomes of each situation.
- ❂ If you have more than one group get each group to feedback their thoughts and solutions.
- ❂ Take comments from the rest of the young people.

Make sure everyone gets a chance to contribute to this discussion.

Handy hints

- ❂ Often these situations will lead onto discussion of real life situations that group members have been in. This may mean disclosure of personal information, so be aware of this prior to starting this exercise. Be aware of relevant child protection guidelines.

Variations

- ❂ These scenarios are also idea for acting out within the group. This allows the opportunity to try out different behaviours, different ways of handling situations involving alcohol and looking at different conclusions to each scenario. These situations were taken from real life examples experienced by young people.

→

Hammered
Young people and alcohol

Drinking scenarios – contd.

Situation 1

You and your pals are at a party and everyone has had a lot to drink. It's after midnight and someone suggests that some of you move on to another party that's going on all night. The problem is that the next party is two miles away. A guy at the party says: "No problem, I've got a car. We can all pile in".

You know he has been drinking a fair bit and seems quite drunk. But you really want to go to the party since someone you fancy will be there. Anyway, there won't be much traffic on the road, and the driver says he will go slowly. You decide to go to the party in the car.

Was this the correct decision to make? Why?
What are the pros and cons of this situation (dangers to self and others, do your parents know where you are, getting into risky situations)?

Situation 2

A group of friends are hanging about in the local park. They are bored – it's the weekend and they have nothing to do. Someone suggested they put all the money that they have together and get someone to get them a carry out of the strongest booze they can get. They end up with a mixture of strong cider and vodka, and spend the rest of the night in the park – until they are completely drunk.

Was this a good way to spend an evening? Why?
Discuss possible situations that might occur (legalities of the situation, drinking outdoors, dangers of being out in the open drunk, getting ill, risky situations, how your parents feel, what happens next, the day after).

Situation 3

A group of friends have been drinking a lot in a park and one of the group has been very sick. She is lying on a park bench, is very pale and freezing cold. People are trying to get her to go home but everyone is completely drunk and afraid of being caught in that condition. She seems to have passed out since no-one can get her to speak anymore. Someone says "We should just leave her here. She'll sober up and get home by herself eventually".

Do you agree with this?
Discuss other ways the situation could be handled (calling ambulance, getting parents).
Discuss the risks involved.

→

Situation 4

At a party you find out that someone is spiking someone else's drink. You don't know the person very well but they don't normally drink and are usually fairly quiet. By now he isn't quiet at all, and people are starting to make jokes and generally make fun of him and the state he is in.

Was this an acceptable thing to do?
Discuss what could or should be done in this case.

Situation 5

A girl has been drinking heavily, and by now she doesn't know what is going on and is totally out of it. You overhear a group of guys discussing who is going to get her into bed first, and generally saying some fairly nasty things about what they will do to her. About fifteen minutes later you see her being led upstairs by one of them. A group of them is laughing as it happens. Your friend says you should go up after her, stop whatever is going to happen, and get her to go home before she does something that she really regrets.

What should you do?
What might happen if you did nothing?
Is it the girl's fault for getting into that state?
Is it an unacceptable situation?

Situation 6

A group of friends are going away on a youth club residential. They have been warned by staff that this is to be an alcohol-free weekend and that anybody found drinking will mean that the group goes home early. Everyone has agreed to this rule and signed a statement to this effect. One of the group is determined that she isn't going away for a weekend without booze, and has taken a bottle of vodka with her. On the first night of the residential, she is offering the bottle around the room you are in, and she is getting very drunk. Someone in the room says they are going to tell a member of staff about this.

Should she tell the member of staff?
What other solutions might there be?
Why might this be a dodgy situation?

→

Situation 7

You are at a family party and everyone is drunk, including your own parents (much to your embarrassment). The problem is that your dad or mum was meant to be the one driving home and they are both way over the limit. At the end of the night you all go to leave and your dad makes for the car and is obviously planning to drive. You say: "No way, let's get a taxi. You're drunk" and a huge row breaks out. To keep the peace, you end up getting into the car anyway, with your dad insisting he has only had a couple anyway.

Was this the right thing to do?
Can you think of ways you could have prevented it happening?

Situation 8

You and a group of friends are going to a rave. You meet up before it to get ready and have a good drink. You have been drinking a fair bit including a couple of lethal vodka and hooch cocktails!! At the rave you are dancing and generally having a good time, but you are pretty out of it and the heat and the last drink you had have really got to you. A friend says she has bought an E and asks if you want half of it. You think "great" and cop it right there in the club.

Was this the right thing to do?
Discuss the possible consequences.
Discuss risky behaviour and how to avoid it.

Situation 9

You are going to a party in a pal's house. The family are away for the weekend and your pal's older sister is planning it. You are excited by this but also a bit scared as there will be lots of older people there and you don't want to look young and immature. Your friend wants you to club together and get a bottle of vodka and lots of strong cider. The problem is that you don't really like drinking much and usually only drink larger. Also she's talking about there being lots of drugs at this party and how it's going to be a wild occasion. You are feeling that everything is getting out of control.

What should you do?
Have you ever felt this way in real life?
Discuss ways of dealing with this.

More case scenarios

Case 1

"A group of us recently went out and missed the bus home. My mate called his dad who came to pick us up. I think he was drunk as he stank of booze. He was mad at us and shouted abuse at us to get in the car. I didn't want to but didn't know what else to do. No-one else said anything. I didn't want to admit I was scared. We all got home ok but his driving was really bad".

What are the underlying issues in this example?
What are the possible consequences of this risk-taking behaviour?
What should you do if this happens again?

Case 2

"I got off with a boy I didn't even know or fancy. We were at the park and this group of older boys we didn't really know had some Cider. My two friends and I got talking to them and they gave us some drink. It didn't take much for us to get really stupid. One of the boys was climbing on the railway lines behind the park and we were singing stupid songs really loudly. One of the boys said he fancied me and started kissing me. Now I feel dirty. I don't want to go near the park again, I'm afraid of seeing him in the street. My friends say it doesn't matter but it does to me. I really hate myself for doing it".

What are the underlying issues in this example?
What are the possible consequences of this risk-taking behaviour?

Case 3

"I used to get on very well with my friends but since the start of 2nd year we all moved classes and mix with a load of people we didn't know before. My friends have joined a group of girls who drink and smoke and they've all started doing it. They probably think I'm an idiot because I don't".

What are the underlying issues in this example?
What are the possible consequences of this risk-taking behaviour?

→

Young people and alcohol

Case 4

"My mum drinks too much. She's been doing it for years. We've covered up for her for ages. No-one else in the family knows about it and neither do any of my friends. Dad has tried to take her to the doctor and to AA but nothing makes a difference. She just keeps drinking and it's ruining all our lives. Now my dad says he's had enough and unless she stops drinking he'll leave- If he goes I don't know what I'll do".

What are the underlying issues in this example?

Case 5

"My best mate won't talk to me. She says it's because I spiked her drink. I don't know why she's so mad. She's been drinking for ages and we always have a laugh. Nothing happened- she just got more drunk than usual. How can I make her see it was just a joke?"

What are the underlying issues in this example?
What are the possible consequences of this risk-taking behaviour?

Hammered
Young people and alcohol

Auntie Hendo: a problem solving exercise

Purpose

- To provide a safe and creative means of raising young people's concerns and questions about alcohol.
- To identify issues for follow up work.
- To show that everyone is able to offer something towards the solution of specific problems, and to demonstrate the potential for group problem solving.
- Problems are presented anonymously but are dealt with openly.
- The exercise is fun and encourages participation- people enjoy writing letters to agony aunts.
- Everyone, even quieter group members, gets a chance to give advice.

Who is it for?

- Any age group.
- Can be used with single-sex groups as well as mixed groups.
- Best with 6-12, but possible to work with larger groups.

Resources and staff required

- A suitable prop to identify Auntie Hendo e.g. wig, flowery hat, outrageous glasses etc (Keep hidden until required).
- A box or similar container.
- Small sheets of paper.
- Pens.
- 1 staff member.

Time allowed

- 5 minutes individual work.
- 25-30 minutes discussions of problems (can go longer).
- 5 minutes feedback.

Instructions

- Explain that the group is to be visited by Auntie Hendo, an agony aunt, who will help with any problems or questions that the group has about alcohol and drinking. You may want to give examples (e.g. "Dear Auntie Hendo, my friend says that they have a better time at parties if you have had a few drinks. What do you think?") Ask each person to write a short letter to Auntie Hendo outlining a problem or question about alcohol, which they would like her to address. Letters should be anonymous or could be signed with a pseudonym like "Worried from Edinburgh". Once written, the letters should be individually folded up and placed into the box. →
- When all the letters have been collected in and shuffled, prepare the group for the arrival of

Hammered
Young people and alcohol

Auntie Hendo: a problem solving exercise - contd.

Auntie Hendo. At this point produce the prop identifying your agony aunt. Explain that everyone will become Auntie Hendo in turn and help to solve the problems written on the letters.

✪ Each person in turn pulls a letter out of the box and looks at it. If it's their own they should place it back in the box and take another. Auntie Hendo then reads the letter aloud and offers constructive advice about dealing with the problem. Once Auntie Hendo is finished giving her piece of advice, other group members are encouraged to add further advice. After everyone has had one or two goes at being Auntie Hendo, check out the issues, which require further discussion.

Handy hints

✪ Encourage quieter Auntie Hendo's to give their opinion.
✪ Ensure confidentiality. Avoid identifying specific writers. Even if the identity can be guessed by the content of the letter, don't aim the response at them.
✪ If factual answers are required, be prepared to provide correct factual information.

Variations

✪ This game is a good way of raising issues for follow up work. A shorter version of the game involves people simply writing the letters without any group discussion. These can then be used by the worker as a way of assessing the group's concerns and questions.

About the Hammered publication

The Hammered publication enclosed inside the front flap of this manual was designed by young people for young people. It is a poster-sized leaflet and was created with a specific audience in mind; young people aged 14-18 years old.

One side of the leaflet is 'a tale of drink sex and violence' based around young people drinking in their under 18s club. It provides facts and includes harm reduction information. The other side is 'Alcohol Affects Everybody', which focuses on useful information about the health consequences of alcohol consumption. Reference is made to various topics such as alcohol absorption, gender and alcohol, the short and long-term effects on the body (Brain, Heart, Kidneys, Liver, and Stomach), alcohol dependency, safe levels and legality issues.

The leaflet is a useful tool which can be used in the youth club setting to stimulate active discussion or formulate issue based workshops.

The Hammered leaflet as a discussion tool

Purpose

- ✪ Encourages young people to read the publication.
- ✪ To allow discussion of issues that young people feel are important in a safe environment.
- ✪ To allow young people to have and express their own views.
- ✪ To begin to explore different attitudes and perceptions about alcohol.

Who is it for?

- ✪ The publication can be used with young people 14-18 years old.

Resources and staff required

- ✪ 1 facilitator per group.
- ✪ Copies of the Hammered leaflet.
- ✪ Flip chart Paper.
- ✪ Flip chart pens.
- ✪ Discussion topics to aid the facilitator.

Time allowed

- ✪ This can vary from 30 minutes-1$\frac{1}{2}$ hours using some of the topics suggested below.

Instructions

- ✪ Hand out the publication and get participants to read it individually.
- ✪ Hand out some A4 paper to allow the young people to note any comments or issues they have thought about as they are reading it.
- ✪ Bring everyone back to form a large group and discuss what people thought of the publication, what bits they liked (characters, storyboard), what information they thought was good/didn't like, was it accurate information? what did they learn from the publication?

Handy hints

- ✪ Try and get as much opinion as possible being expressed.
- ✪ Use the topics as a starting point and let the discussion flow from there.
- ✪ Everyone should get the chance to speak and be heard!
- ✪ Get to know people's names before you start so you can direct questions at individuals. Asking questions to the whole group may result in having only one or two people answering all the time.
- ✪ Be safe, that is, ask questions in such a way that people are comfortable, and don't expose anyone's personal use. Ask indirect questions, e.g. "What kind of alcoholic drinks do young people consume?" "Where do young people drink?"
- ✪ Be aware of the quiet ones in your group. It may be that they need to be asked and are not comfortable putting their opinion forward.

Hammered
Young people and alcohol

Discussion topics

Explore how and why young people start drinking

Ask the group about first time use:

- How old they were when they first tried alcohol?
- What drinks did they try first?
- Why they first tried alcohol?
- Why young people start to drink?
- How do young people get a hold of alcohol?
- First drinking experience… Where were you, who were you with?…

What are young people expectations of drinking?

Ask the group:

- What did they think it would be like?
- What did/do they hope to get out of it?
- What actually happens?
- Are the effects what was expected?

What are adults views of drinking?

Ask the group about:

- How do adults they know (parents/carers/teachers etc.) drink?
- What do the adults/parents they know think of young people drinking?
- What do they think of the adults views?
- Are adult views hypocritical?
- What do they know about alcohol and the law?

When do we drink?

Have a discussion around cultural aspects of drinking:

- When does drinking happen? (e.g. weddings, New Year, weekends, parties)
- What is the purpose of drinking at these events?

Explore what people drink

Ask the group about:

- What type of drinks they consume?
- How much do they drink?
- How does this differ from adult drinking patterns?

→

Hammered
Young people and alcohol

Explore safer places to drink

Ask the group:

- Where do young people drink and why?
- Where do adults drink and why?
- What is a safe place to drink?
- What are the pros and cons of drinking in different settings?

Explore drinking and driving

Ask the group:

- What is a unit of alcohol?
- How much alcohol is a safe level for driving?
- What are the issues of being a passenger in a car where the driver has been drinking?
- How do you refuse a lift?

Explore young people's views

Ask the group:

- At what age should young people be allowed to drink?
- What is the current legal age for consuming alcohol?
- How does this fit in with other age related laws?
- How does the law regulate consumption and sale of alcohol?

Consider the positives and negatives of drinking

Ask the group:

- What do they get out of drinking? (Dutch courage, look cool etc.)
- What is the negative side of drinking? (health, violence, promiscuity, STIs, making a fool of yourself etc.)

Gender issues

Ask the group

- Do men and women use and view alcohol in the same way?
- Why do girls drink?
- Why do boys drink?
- What do girls think of drunk boys and vice versa?

Think about: the derogatory language used to describe women when they are drunk. Is this the same for boys?

→

Hammered
Young people and alcohol

Explore peer pressure

Ask the group:

- Do they feel pressure to drink if others in their peer group do?
- Why?
- Is it easy (or not) to resist peer pressure?
- How can you deal with this?

Look at the links of alcohol use and violence in more depth

Ask the group:

- To tell you about incidents of violence they have experienced or heard about.
- What is the connection between alcohol and violence?
- What are their concerns for their safety whilst drinking?
- Are women and men equally likely to become violent/victims after drinking?

How much is too much?

Ask the group:

- What is safe consumption of alcohol?
- Should/does this vary according to age and gender?
- How do you know when you have had too much alcohol?
- What are the long-term effects of alcohol misuse?
- When does the damage to health begin?
- What are the danger signs?
- How do you become dependent on alcohol?

Pass on the Harm Reduction Message

Ask the group:

- What they can do to make drinking a safer pastime.

Pass on the information:

- Eat plenty first.
- Pace yourself with soft drinks or water in-between alcoholic drinks.
- Avoid mixing drinks.
- Watch out for people spiking drinks.
- Look after each other.
- Drink some water when you get home. There are no hangover cures apart from time. →

Hammered
Young people and alcohol

Teach them how to put someone in the recovery position. Young people can find learning first aid interesting as well as a fun exercise.

Variations

- Each of the topics can be used to devise group work (workshops), which can be delivered over a series of weeks.

References

Alcohol Concern (2001) *Alcohol and Mental Health.* London, Alcohol Concern.

Alcohol Concern (2000) *Britain's Ruin? Alcohol's Role in Social Exclusion.* London, Alcohol Concern.

Alcohol Focus Scotland www.alcohol-focus-scotland.org.uk

Brewers and Licensed Retailers Association (2000) *Brewers Society Statistical Handbook.* London, BLRA. www.blra.co.uk

Currie, C. (1998) *Health Behaviour of Scottish Schoolchildren Survey.* Edinburgh University.

Department of Health (2002) *Smoking, drinking and drug use among young people in 2001: Preliminary Results.* www.doh.gov.uk/public/sddsurvey01.htm

Department of Health (2001a) *Statistical Bulletin: Statistics on Alcohol – England, 1978 Onwards.* Statistical Bulletin 2001/3, London, HMSO.

Department of Health (2001b) *Annual Report of the Chief Medical Officer of the Department of Health 2001.* London, DoH.

Department of Health (1995) *Sensible Drinking. The Report of Inter-Departmental Working Group.* London, DoH.

Department for Transport (2001) *Road Accidents Great Britain 2001: The Casualty Report.* London, The Stationery Office.

Drinkwise www.drinkwise.co.uk

DTLR (2003) *Road Accident Great Britain: 2002.* The Casualty Report.

Ettore, E. (1997) *Women and Alcohol: A Private Pleasure or Public Problem?* Women's Press.

Fast Forward (1999) *Skoosh.* Health Education Board for Scotland.

General Register Office for Scotland (GROS) *Drug Related Deaths in Scotland in 2000.* www.gro-scotland.gov.uk/grosweb

Harrison, L. (1999) 'Do the Rich Really Die Young? Alcohol-Related Mortality and Social Class in Great Britain, 1988-1994'. *Addiction.* 94: 12, 1871-80.

Healthy Living and NHS Health Scotland (2004) *Alcohol. What Every Parent Should Know.* Health Scotland.

Health Education Board for Scotland (2000) *Indicators for Health in Scotland. Summary of Findings from the 1998 Health Education Population Survey.* Health Education Board for Scotland.

Home Office (1998) *The 1998 British Crime Survey, England and Wales, Home Office Statistical Bulletin Issue 21/98.* London, Research, Development and Statistics.

Kershaw, C. (2000) *The 2000 British Crime Survey, England and Wales.* London, Home Office Research, Development and Statistics Directorate.

National Statistics (2003) *Health Statistics Quarterly 17.* Spring, The Stationery Office, London. www.statistics.gov.uk/products/p6725.asp

National Statistics (2003) *Statistics on Alcohol: England.* Statistical Bulletin. www.statistics.gov.uk

National Statistics (2000) *Psychiatric Morbidity Among Adults, 2000.* www.statistics.gov.uk

Office for National Statistics ONS (2001) *Living in Britain: Results from the 1998 General Household Survey.* London, The Stationery Office.

Office for National Statistics (2000) *Mortality Statistics: Cause, England and Wales, 1999.* London, The Stationery Office.

Office for National Statistics (2000) *Family Spending. A Report on the 1999-2000 Family Expenditure Survey.* London, The Stationery Office.

Plant, Martin (Ed.) (1997) *Alcohol: Minimising the Harm: What Works?* Free Association Books.

Plant, Moira (1997) *Women and Alcohol: Contemporary and Historical Perspectives.* Free Association Books.

The Portman Group (2000) *Alcohol and Society; Research Conducted by MORI for the Portman Group Pt1: General Attitudes.* London. www.portman-group.org.uk

Potter, K. (2002) *Consultation With Children and Young People on the Scottish Executive's Plan for Action on Alcohol Misuse.*

Research Collaboratory for Structural Bioinformatics (RCSB) (2001) *Alcohol Dehydrogenase.* Protein Data Bank. www.rcsb.org/pdb/molecules/pdb13_1.html

Scottish Executive (2003) *Alcohol Misuse in Scotland: Trends and Costs: Final Report.* www.scotland.gov.uk/health/alcoholproblems/docs/trco-03.asp

Scottish Executive (2001) *Road Accidents Scotland*, 2000. Scottish Executive.

Scottish Executive (2000). *Scottish Health Survey 1998.* www.show.scot.nhs.uk/scottishhealthsurvey

Statistics on Alcohol in Scotland. www.scotland.gov.uk/health/alcohol problems/docs/paap1-00.asp

Strategy Unit Alcohol Harm Reduction Project. *National Alcohol Harm Reduction Strategy (2003) Interim Analysis.* Executive Summary. www.number10.gov.uk/files/pdf/al-consummary.pdf

SHEU (1997) *Young People and Alcohol. Attitudes to Drinking 1983-2001.* www.sheu.org.uk/pubs/ypalc.htm

Walker, A. et al. (2001) *Living in Britain: Results From the 2000 General Household Survey.* London, The Stationery Office.

Whent, H. (1997) *Health Update: Alcohol.* HEA.

World Health Organisation (2002) *The World Health Report 2002: Reducing Risks, Promoting Healthy Life.* World Health Organisation.

Fact Sheets

Alcohol Concern Fact Sheets www.alcoholconcern.org.uk

(1996) *Sensible Drinking Limits*

(2001) *Alcohol and Crime*

(2001) *Alcoholism or Problem Drinking*

(2001) *Alcohol and the UK Law*

(2001) *Alcopops*

(2001) *Binge Drinking*

(2002) *Alcohol and Pregnancy*

(2002) *Drink Drive Accidents*

(2003) *Advertising and Alcohol*

(2003) *Alcohol and Men*

(2003) *Alcohol Drinking Among Black and Minority Ethnic (BME) Communities in the United Kingdom*

(2003) *Health Impacts of Alcohol*

(2003) *Women and Alcohol*

(2003) *Young People and Alcohol*

(2004) *Women and Alcohol*

Institute of Alcohol Studies (IAS) Fact Sheets www.ias.org.uk

(2003) *Alcohol and Crime*

(2003) *Alcohol-related Crime and Disorder*

(2003) *Drinking and Driving*

(2004) *Alcohol and Health*

(2004) *Young People and Alcohol*